Computer-Assisted Reporting

A Practical Guide

Third Edition

Brant Houston
Investigative Reporters and Editors, Inc.
University of Missouri, Columbia

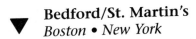

Bedford/St. Martin's
Boston • New York

To Rhonda

For Bedford/St. Martin's

Developmental Editor: Vikram Mukhija
Assistant Editor, Publishing Services: Maria Burwell
Senior Production Supervisor: Joe Ford
Production Associate: Christie Gross
Marketing Manager: Richard Cadman
Project Management: Books By Design, Inc.
Text Design: Books By Design, Inc.
Cover Design: Lucy Krikorian
Cover Art: George B. Diebold/CORBIS
Composition: Books By Design, Inc.
Printing and Binding: RR Donnelley & Sons Company

President: Joan E. Feinberg
Editorial Director: Denise B. Wydra
Publisher for History and Communication: Patricia A. Rossi
Director of Marketing: Karen Melton Soeltz
Director of Editing, Design, and Production: Marcia Cohen
Manager, Publishing Services: Emily Berleth

Library of Congress Control Number: 2003103954

Manufactured in the United States of America.

9 8 7 6 5 4
f e d c b a

For information, write:
Bedford/St. Martin's, 75 Arlington Street, Boston, MA 02116
(617-399-4000)

ISBN: 0-312-41149-9

Acknowledgments

Acknowledgments and copyrights appear at the back of the book on page 241, which constitutes an extension of the copyright page.

▷ **Preface**

Unlike many textbooks that discuss computer-assisted reporting (CAR), the practical guide you are holding in your hands is based on nearly two decades of data analysis and news reporting experience. I did not begin using CAR because I was captivated by computers or data, but because in the 1980s, more government and business information was being delivered in digital formats than in hard copy. In order to get that information, I had to learn new skills — CAR skills. Learning those skills improved my reporting and increased my credibility.

As Executive Director of Investigative Reporters and Editors and the National Institute for Computer-Assisted Reporting, I have overseen more than 300 CAR seminars and conferences and taught more than 150 personally, in print and broadcast, for students and professional journalists. As a result, this book's step-by-step approach to CAR is continually "road-tested," and has been improved over three editions by listening to suggestions from teachers, students, professionals and you, the reader.

The third edition of "Computer-Assisted Reporting" continues to provide students with the data collection and analysis skills that they need to report and write better news stories. As introduced in this book, the basics of computer-assisted reporting — finding data on the Internet, using spreadsheets and/or database managers to analyze it, building databases, cleaning dirty data and writing the computer-assisted news story — can help beginning and experienced journalists work with greater speed and insight. At the same computer at which they learned CAR, students will be able to develop stories that, for instance, compare income levels in a community, identify high crime areas, examine pollution records and track the data that lead to compelling stories.

"Computer-Assisted Reporting" can be used as a core text or as a supplement to any introductory or intermediate journalism textbook. In recognition of CAR's now widespread practice, this edition features a new organization that parallels the reporting and writing process taught in most journalism courses. As a result, instructors can more easily incorporate lessons on CAR skills into courses that cover a variety of essential news reporting and writing skills.

▼ Features

Because computer-assisted reporting is only as good as the stories it produces, this third edition includes more reporting and writing advice for using CAR skills in daily and beat reporting. Other key features of "Computer-Assisted Reporting" have been retained and strengthened:

- A practical approach helps students master the basics of computer-assisted reporting, teaching them the essential skills they need in concise, accessible language.
- Illustrated instructions and examples from common software such as Microsoft Excel, Access and Explorer let students match what they see in the book to what they see on their screens and confirm their results.
- Real-life news stories written with the aid of computer-assisted reporting techniques — such as investigating police shootings in Washington, D.C., health violations in St. Paul's restaurants or school bus routes in rural West Virginia — show students the utility and power of CAR skills.
- "Your Turn to Practice" exercises provide realistic and engaging assignments that give students an opportunity to practice the skills they just learned.
- Professional's Appendixes give brief introductions to choosing hardware and software, and advanced CAR skills such as statistical analysis, mapping data and analyzing social relationships.

▼ New to This Edition

To keep pace with changing journalistic practice and help students clearly see how to apply CAR skills, the third edition has been thoroughly revised, updated and reorganized to focus on how to accurately and ethically turn data into sources, story ideas and finished stories. In addition, two new chapters on the uses of spreadsheets and database managers expand the basic skills instruction, more than any other CAR textbook.

Several other significant changes to the third edition are:

- "CAR Wars" features and epigrams, drawn from the National Institute of Computer-Assisted Reporting's newsletter Uplink, tell true stories of why working journalists learned to do CAR — and how they succeeded.
- An updated and expanded chapter on researching and downloading data from the Internet (Chapter 2).
- An additional chapter on spreadsheets with more instruction in day-to-day skills (Chapter 4).
- An additional chapter on database managers with more on relational databases and the use of Structured Query Language for data analysis (Chapter 6).
- An expanded chapter devoted to building databases, a practice that is becoming more commonplace (Chapter 8).
- An expanded chapter on using CAR in news stories and more examples on how journalists have used CAR for stories (Chapter 10).
- Bolded key terms defined in the glossary and an updated bibliography of select CAR resources round out the usefulness of "Computer-Assisted Reporting" for a student's entire career.

"Computer-Assisted Reporting" is supplemented with an updated Web site that includes chapter exercises, datasets, brief supplementary tutorials and links to related online sources at IRE and NICAR. The site —**www.ire.org/carbook** — was built to keep "Computer-Assisted Reporting" updated until its next revision.

▼ Acknowledgments

I thank Investigative Reporters and Editors Inc. (IRE), the Missouri School of Journalism and Dean Mills for providing support for computer-assisted reporting; Steve Weinberg, former executive director of IRE and professor at the Missouri School of Journalism, and deputy director Len Bruzzese for their support and encouragement; the current and former staff at IRE and the National Institute for Computer-Assisted Reporting (NICAR); former NICAR trainers Ron Nixon, Aron Pilhofer, Jennifer LaFleur, Neil Reisner, Sarah Cohen, Tom McGinty, Jo Craven McGinty, Jeff Porter and David Herzog; my former academic colleague Richard Mullins; and all the journalists and students who have made helpful suggestions, especially Ron Campbell, Andy Hall and David Milliron.

I appreciate the suggestions and help provided by Arin Stark, Jack Dolan, Justin Mayo and John Sullivan on previous editions. I also want to thank Philip Meyer and Dwight Morris, first-generation CAR journalists and mentors, who continue to be an inspiration to me. I owe thanks to Elliot Jaspin for starting in 1989 the organization that has become NICAR and setting the high standards for NICAR's work.

I would also like to thank reviewers of the third edition: David Armstrong, Boston University; Daniel Berkowitz, University of Iowa; Ronald Campbell, The Orange County Register; Ira Chinoy, University of Maryland; Richard Gordon, Northwestern University; Charles H. Green, Florida International University; Shelton Gunaratne, Minnesota State University; Jerry Reynolds, Humboldt State University; and Lawrence Schneider, California State University, Northridge.

And many, many thanks to Bedford/St. Martin's, particularly Patricia Rossi, publisher; Vikram Mukhija, editor; Alice Mack, editorial assistant; and Richard Cadman, marketing manager — all of whom have put tremendous work into this revision. Also, many thanks to Nancy Benjamin of Books By Design for her work on this edition.

One final word. Despite the power and breadth of CAR, it remains only a tool for journalists. It aids, but does not replace, the imagination, experience, interviewing skills, intuition, skepticism, "shoe leather" work and passion of the dedicated journalist, whom I acknowledge here last but not least.

Brant Houston

▷ Contents

CHAPTER **10**

CHAPTER 1

High-Tech Journalism

What Computer-Assisted Reporting Is and Why Journalists Use It

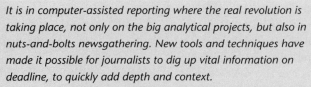

It is in computer-assisted reporting where the real revolution is taking place, not only on the big analytical projects, but also in nuts-and-bolts newsgathering. New tools and techniques have made it possible for journalists to dig up vital information on deadline, to quickly add depth and context.

— "We're All Nerds Now," Joel Simon and Carol Napolitano,
The Columbia Journalism Review

You are researching how many inmates are in state jails because they can't come up with the money for bail. The regular court reporter tells you that he believes many people are in jail not because they were convicted of a crime but because they didn't have the necessary finances to be free while awaiting trial. Furthermore, the reporter thinks judges are setting higher bails for black and Hispanic males than for white males.

With a little investigation, you discover that the court system keeps records on the bail set for each case in the state. There is, however, a catch: There are 150,000 records, and parts of each are confidential.

Court officials expect and hope that you will request thousands of sheets of paper and then wait months for them to blacken out confidential information. They plan to charge you thousands of dollars that your newspaper probably won't pay.

They assume you will give up on the story or, at best, come up with only anecdotal evidence that they can easily refute.

But you have an answer. You agree to take the records, not on paper but in the form of an electronic database.

After a series of meetings, the officials agree to give you the database with the information you need. It turns out that it's easy to delete the confidential information on an electronic database, and the cost is reduced to less than $100.

In the morning you pick up a CD-ROM containing the database, and in the afternoon you transfer the information to your personal computer. By the next morning, using store-bought software, you have completed your first analysis of the data and have discovered that the bail for black and Hispanic males is usually double that for whites, even when they are charged with the same crime and have the same criminal and personal backgrounds.

Over the next few weeks, you examine the records further and gather more details. You recheck your information, consult other documents, conduct interviews, and write the story. The work culminates in a front-page story that presents a systematic look at justice gone wrong. The officials' best rebuttal is that the system discriminates against poor males, not black and Hispanic males.

Now consider this more recent scenario.

You want to know how weak the security is at your nearby metropolitan airport. You download recent information from the Federal Aviation Administration Web site or ask the National Institute for Computer-Assisted Reporting (**www.nicar.org**) to ship you the complete FAA database, which the institute routinely downloads and distributes.

You begin analyzing the database, which consists of counting the number of violations at your local airport in recent years and then closely examining the details of those violations.

You quickly find many serious and surprising violations in which people successfully brought guns, knives and other weapons through security. You follow up with research on the Web and interviews with airport officials, law enforcement agencies, and airline companies. Finally, you examine reports from government investigators that are posted on the Web. Within 24 hours, you have an important story that the public needs to know.

Both of these scenarios really happened, one on the local level and one on the national level. In fact, more than 100 news organizations used information from databases for their articles on airport security in the weeks following the terrorists' attacks on September 11, 2001.

The techniques described in the preceding scenarios are called **computer-assisted reporting** and are a part of everyday journalism. Journalists use these and other methods for daily reporting, reporting on the beat and for the large projects that win Pulitzer Prizes. In the past decade, prizes have gone to The Washington Post for stories on police shootings and child abuse; Newsday for its investigation of an airliner crash; and The News and Observer in Raleigh, N.C., for a probe into the hog farm industry.

No student or beginning journalist should be without these skills.

Computer-assisted reporting does not refer to journalists sitting at a keyboard, writing stories or surfing the Web. It requires downloading databases and analyzing data, critical thinking and thoughtful online research that can provide context and depth to daily stories. It includes techniques of producing tips that launch more complex stories from a broader perspective and with better, in-depth understanding of the issues. The journalist who begins a story with the knowledge of the patterns gleaned from 150,000 court records is way ahead of the reporter who sees only a handful of court cases each week.

Computer-assisted reporting hasn't replaced proven journalistic practices but has become a part of them. It also requires greater responsibility and vigilance. The old standard "Verify, verify, verify," which one learns in basic reporting classes, becomes even more critical. "Healthy skepticism" becomes more important, and the practice of interviewing multiple sources and cross-referencing them is more crucial.

"Computers don't make a bad reporter into a good reporter. What they do is make a good reporter better," Elliot Jaspin, one of the pioneers in computer-assisted reporting, said more than a decade ago.

Over the past ten years, many practicing journalists have sought training and become proficient in the basic skills of computer-assisted reporting. They overcame computer and math phobias and now use those skills on a daily basis, with the result of more precise and sophisticated reporting. To quote Philip Meyer, a pioneer in database analysis for news stories, "They are raising the ante on what it takes to be a journalist."

Aiding in the progress and acceptance of these skills has been the proliferation of the Web, the development of inexpensive and easy-to-use computers and software and the increased use of these techniques in newsrooms. Data analysis that once required a mainframe computer or a high-powered and high-priced personal computer can now be done on any laptop or home computer.

Computer-assisted reporting is no longer just a sidebar to mainstream journalism but is essential to surviving as a journalist in the 21st century. The tools of computer-assisted reporting won't replace a good journalist's imagination, the ability to conduct revealing interviews or the talent to develop sources. But a journalist who knows how to use computers in day-to-day and long-term work will gather and analyze information more quickly, provide more context and develop and deliver a deeper understanding of the story's subject. The journalist will be better prepared for interviews, able to write with more authority and discover stories that he or she would have never otherwise considered.

The journalist also will achieve parity with politicians, bureaucrats and businessmen who have enjoyed many advantages over the Fourth Estate simply because they had the money and knowledge to utilize computers and electronic information before journalists did. Government officials and workers are generally quite comfortable entering information into computers and then retrieving and analyzing it. Businesses, small and large, routinely use spreadsheet and database software, and advocacy groups frequently employ databases to push their agendas.

Without a rudimentary knowledge of the advantages and disadvantages of computers, it is difficult for the contemporary journalist to understand and report on how the world works today. And it is far more difficult for a journalist to do meaningful public service journalism or to perform the necessary watchdog role.

As long ago as 1990, Frank Daniels III, former executive editor of the Raleigh News & Observer, recognized the challenge. He began his newspaper's early and oft-lauded push into computer-assisted reporting because the 1990 campaign of then-Senator Jesse Helms was profoundly more computer-sophisticated than Daniels' own newspaper. "It made me realize how stupid we were, and I don't like feeling stupid," Daniels recalled.

Daniels was right about the bad position in which journalists had put themselves. For years, journalists were like animals in a zoo, waiting to be fed pellets of information by the keepers who were just as happy for journalists to stay in their Luddite cages. But a good journalist wants to see the original information because every time someone else selects or sorts that information, that person can add a spin or bias that can't be detected. Computer-assisted reporting can help prevent that from happening.

Many journalists and journalism students now learn the basic tools of computer-assisted reporting because they realize it is the best way to access information, since most governmental and commercial records are now stored electronically. Despite security concerns, there are still a mind-boggling number of databases on U.S. government and international Web sites. So without the ability to deal with electronic data, a journalist is cut off from some of the best, untainted information. The old-fashioned journalist will never get to the information on time or, worse, will be trampled by competing media.

Such knowledge is also crucial for the journalist or journalism student who is seeking employment. At many news organizations, the applicant with these skills will outshine the competition.

A journalist who can use a spreadsheet or database manager is free to thoroughly explore information, reexamine it and reconsider what it means in relation to interviews and observations in the field. The journalist can take the "spin" off the information and get closer to the truth. A journalist may not be a statistician, but a good journalist knows enough about statistics to appreciate how easy it is to manipulate or distort them. In the same way, if a journalist understands how data can be manipulated, he or she can better judge a bureaucrat's spin on the facts or a government's misuse of a database.

Journalists have come to understand, too, that if they allow the person who processes the data to also do the analysis, they may overlook the data's nuances or potential pitfalls. A data processor does not think like a journalist either; what may be significant to the journalist may seem unimportant to the data processor. Using a data processor to do all the work is like asking someone else to read a book for you.

The conscientious journalist does not want to fall into a cycle of requesting a printout, studying it, asking more questions, and then asking for another printout. Why get into a lengthy back-and-forth when you can engage in a rapid, multidimensioned conversation with the data on your computer screen?

Most important, computer-assisted reporting is at the heart of public service journalism and of vigilant daily reporting whether in education, business, government, environment or any other topic.

▼ History of Computer-Assisted Reporting

Many practitioners date the beginning of computer-assisted reporting to 1952 when CBS tried to use experts with a mainframe computer to predict the outcome of the presidential election. That's a bit of a stretch, or perhaps it was just a false beginning because it wasn't until 1967 that data analysis started to catch on.

In that year Philip Meyer at the Detroit Free Press used a mainframe to analyze a survey of Detroit residents for the purpose of understanding and explaining the serious riots that had erupted in the city that summer.

In the 1970s, Meyer went on to work with Philadelphia Inquirer reporters Donald Barlett and James Steele to analyze the sentencing patterns in the local court system and with Rich Morin at The Miami Herald to analyze property assessment records. Meyer also wrote a book called "Precision Journalism" that explained and advocated using database analysis and social research methods in reporting.

Still, only a few journalists used these techniques before the mid-1980s, when Elliot Jaspin of the Providence Journal Bulletin received recognition for analyzing databases for stories, including those on dangerous school bus drivers and a political scandal involving home loans. At the same time, other journalists across the country, often consulting with Meyer or Jaspin, began doing data analysis for their stories.

Aiding their efforts were improved personal computers and a program — Nine-Track Express — that Jaspin and journalist-programmer Daniel Woods wrote to make it easier to transfer computer tapes (that contain nine "tracks" of information) to personal computers, using a portable tape drive. This allowed journalists to circumvent the bureaucracies and delays involved in using mainframes.

In 1989, the profession recognized the value of computer-assisted reporting when it gave a Pulitzer Prize to the Atlanta Journal-Constitution for its stories on racial disparities in home loan practices. During the same year, Jaspin established the institute at the Missouri School of Journalism, now known as NICAR, and in 1990, Indiana University professor James Brown held the first computer-assisted reporting conference in Indianapolis.

Over the past decade, the use of computer-assisted reporting has blossomed, primarily due to the seminars conducted at Missouri and throughout the world by Investigative Reporters and Editors Inc. and NICAR, which is a joint program of IRE and the Missouri School of Journalism.

▼ The Basic Tools

Since the early 1990s, three basic **tools** (which are the focus of this book) for computer-assisted reporting have emerged: online resources, spreadsheets and database managers. As journalists have become more technologically sophisticated, other tools have joined these three, such as statistical software and GIS (geographical information systems), or **mapping software.**

In providing training to thousands of journalists since 1989, NICAR has found that the beginning journalist in computer-assisted reporting starts most comfortably with the first three tools.

Online resources are available to journalists who can contact another computer through a modem or a network in which computers are already linked. Online resources include (1) electronic mail (e-mail), (2) discussion groups and (3) database libraries, where records are stored. With online resources you can look up court records, retrieve campaign records or the national budgets of countries, connect into your local city hall or find experts a continent away.

Spreadsheet software such as Microsoft Excel is good for analyzing numbers. You should think about using a spreadsheet whenever you are looking at salaries, budgets, census data, prices or statistical reports. A spreadsheet allows you to quickly sum columns of numbers, compare them, sort them and put your results into charts. Of course, you can do much more with a spreadsheet, but for basic computer-assisted reporting, these are routine uses.

A *database manager* such as Microsoft Access is good for searching, summarizing and relating different files. It can keep track of sources, working much better than a paper Rolodex or index cards. A database manager can group similar kinds of information and link different files through key words or identification numbers. It enables you to look up information about a person by name, street address or phone number. You can locate political contributions to a particular candidate and group and total them. It enables you to match the names in one file of information, such as death certificates, to names in another file, such as voters. (There's always a potential story when you find dead people voting.) A database manager can handle many more records than a spreadsheet because spreadsheets technically are limited to about 64,000 records. As a practical matter, working with more than a few thousand records in a spreadsheet can be awkward.

The following are some of the more advanced tools of computer-assisted reporting.

Statistical software (SPPS or SAS are two common brands) becomes attractive later when a journalist feels more comfortable with numbers and wants to perform more detailed analysis such as regression analysis. Journalists use it for examining topics such as school testing scores or racial disparities in mortgages or insurance.

GIS or *mapping software* (most often ArcView, distributed by the company ESRI) illustrates specific points made in a story and illuminates disclosures that otherwise would remain hidden. Journalists often use it for tracking campaign finance and election votes, dangerous environmental areas and many other topics. One famous use involved the red and blue election map by USA Today in the year 2000. The newspaper color-coded counties according to which presidential candidate — Bush or Gore —the county voted for. Comedians even used the map for jokes about the election.

Social networking software. Journalists are just discovering this software, which visually draws connections between people and/or organizations. Anthropologists, business consultants, intelligence and police agencies and health researchers are already using this software to explore and expose relationships.

Computer-assisted reporting uses other tools, some of which are complex and some of which are merely handy. Certainly, more advanced journalists are using — when appropriate — statistical software, GIS software and social networking software, but this book concentrates on the basic tools and analysis that will help you get started in a classroom or a newsroom. This book strips away the distractions (like computer manuals) that can be overwhelming when you begin learning how to use software, and it shows you shortcuts to writing effective stories. The book also presents the use of software in the context of journalism and day-to-day reporting.

▼ Trial and Error, and Repetition

The best way to learn computer-assisted reporting is through trial and error. *You have to practice.* You have to make mistakes when asking questions about the information. You need to try different queries in database managers, look at the results and try again to see if you can better focus your inquiry and the answers to it. You need to be intellectually daring and creative to think of the variables that could affect a conclusion.

The exercises that accompany this book, which can be found on the Web at **www.ire.org/carbook,** will give you plenty of opportunities to try different ways of arranging data and finding valid answers. Moreover, you must realize that despite all the software advances, computer software still has quirks, multiple icons and obscure keystrokes. Practice is the best way to become more comfortable with the tools.

▼ Where You're Going

Part I, "Learning Computer-Assisted Reporting Skills," concentrates on basic skills, whereas Part II, "Using Computer-Assisted Reporting in News Stories," focuses on producing computer-assisted stories and overcoming common newsgathering problems that occur when you use these skills.

The first section concentrates on learning the basic computer-assisted reporting skills for sorting, filtering and summarizing data. These skills include downloading data from the **Internet** and importing it into spreadsheets and database managers; using math, charts and other tools in spreadsheets to analyze data; and using database managers to search, summarize and compare databases.

The second section focuses on writing stories with computer-assisted reporting and dealing with all the practical challenges of finding and negotiating for data, cleaning up dirty data, building a database when there isn't one and weaving it altogether to produce better news stories.

Chapter 2 offers tips for using search engines (e.g., Google) on the Web for datasets, using e-mail discussions groups and downloading data. In recent years, many public databases have been uploaded to the Web. This means a journalist doing computer-assisted reporting can get useful data without having to go through the frequently painful process of requesting it from officials.

This chapter lists some of the most common Web sites and indexes from which to obtain data. It also discusses the columns and rows format of a data table, the challenges with downloading the data and judging the accuracy of data.

Once a journalist has downloaded data to the computer, he or she can do some basic analysis and browsing. Chapter 3 introduces the spreadsheet, which most journalists agree is the fundamental tool for starting out in computer-assisted analysis. Spreadsheets also are a good way for a journalist to get comfortable with basic math, and many of the examples show how math is applied to cut through the "spin" that politicians or bureaucrats can put on numbers.

Chapter 4 deals with the more advanced uses of spreadsheets that filter, reshape and visualize and interpret data. This chapter introduces the concept of grouping and counting records. The chapter also presents some basic charts and graphs that a spreadsheet can produce to make numbers more understandable. This chapter serves as a bridge to the next chapter on database managers by discussing the similarities of data analysis in spreadsheets and database managers.

Chapter 5 describes the basics of database managers, which can be a bit more difficult to learn but are the logical next step in data analysis after using spreadsheets. Database managers are frequently used for grouping categories of records and for linking one file of information to another. They do these tasks much more powerfully and handle many more records than a spreadsheet can.

Database managers allow you to quickly select columns of information, filter in or filter out certain kinds of information, group some items together and then order the results. In addition, you may link one file of information in a database to another or do what is sometimes called matchmaking. Chapter 5 focuses on learning searching and grouping techniques. This chapter uses the "query by example" interface provided by the software Microsoft Access.

Chapter 6 continues with the application of database managers for journalism and shows how to link files. This chapter uses Structured Query Language, also known as SQL. While SQL might seem a bit intimidating, it is often a more rapid and intuitive way of examining data for stories. If a journalist knows SQL, he or she can quickly learn and use any database manager, which can be helpful as software rapidly evolves.

Part II deals with the pursuit of the news story and the challenges a journalist faces in doing so. Chapter 7 discusses strategies for obtaining data that officials may be reluctant to distribute but that may be much more detailed and useful. Laws that have only begun to catch up with technology, and security and privacy concerns, pose barriers to obtaining databases. This chapter examines some of the common obstacles presented by bureaucrats and commercial vendors and advises you on how to get around them. The chapter also looks at methods for finding the right database for the story, requesting the data and negotiating for data for a reasonable price within a reasonable time.

Chapter 8 presents the steps for creating your own databases when a government won't release them or when they don't exist. This chapter is intended especially for journalists and student journalists in small communities in the United States and other countries whose governments or campuses do not make databases available or do not collect information electronically.

Chapter 9 discusses "dirty data." Dirty data is an incomplete or incorrect database that must be "cleaned" — that is, completed or corrected. Most, if not all, databases contain errors (just like newspapers and broadcast reports). A journalist needs to know how to find those errors and either correct them or note them. The cleaning up of dirty data can become complex, but Chapter 9 discusses some of the basic methods.

In Chapter 10, we talk about strategies for finding and getting started on computer-assisted stories and how *not* to get lost in the abundance of information and possibilities. We look at the steps that make up computer-assisted reporting and how to effectively write a story that uses computer-assisted reporting techniques. We review examples and methods to ensure that numbers don't overwhelm a story and how to verify that the anecdotal material is representative of the trends and facts discovered while doing data analysis. The chapter also contains advice for editors and news directors on how to manage and supervise computer-assisted reporting.

The appendixes to this book are aimed at both students and professionals, practicing journalists taking the next step after the basics. Both groups need to be aware of the more advanced tools. Among the topics covered are choosing equipment and software, using statistics and statistical software, GIS (or mapping software) and social networking software.

▼ Practical Advice

Computer-assisted reporting is always a new adventure with a multitude of possibilities and outcomes. This handbook does not attempt to cover everything, but it offers enough practical advice to jump-start the hesitant student or journalist into using it for daily, beat or long-term reporting.

One final thought before we get started: A journalist's success in learning computer-assisted reporting depends on that journalist's own efforts no matter how difficult or frustrating it is or how much CAR may drive you crazy. It's like the old vaudeville joke:

A man goes to a doctor and says, "My brother is making me crazy."
The doctor asks why, and the man says, "Because my brother thinks he's a chicken."
The doctor says, "Well, tell him he's not a chicken."
"But, Doc," says the man, "I need the eggs."

Face it. You need the eggs.

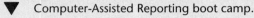

▼ CAR Wars

▼ Analyzing city employee salaries for a story on pay equity was
▼ reinforced by three lessons I learned at the National Institute for
▼ Computer-Assisted Reporting boot camp.

▼ 1. Do your homework.
     2. Get everything.
▼   3. Guarantee a "minimum" story.

When I approached the personnel directors in cities in the Salt Lake
area, they told me they could give me a *range* of salaries but not
the exact earnings of individual employees. However, I knew from
researching my state's open records laws that salaries had to be dis-
closed.

I learned the hard way about getting everything. I had only
asked for employee names, salaries and job titles. I soon realized I
also needed tenure and the city department in which an employee
worked. I ended up going back to the cities. I also had neglected
to push for record layouts and code sheets. In this case, I was able
to work through the problems.

Finally, I learned the value of "the minimum story." The most
obvious finding — and the easiest story to write — was that female
employees were very scarce in top management. I pursued that
angle and found that women who get the same jobs as men
earned comparable salaries, but the hang-up was that few women
crossed the line from traditional female jobs to traditional male
jobs, including top management.

Edward Carter, The Deseret News in Utah

 ## Chapter Checklist

• Journalists need to know how to search for and analyze information on computers because governments and businesses are using
computers to store and distribute information. It also is a skill
that is needed to compete with other news organizations or to get
better jobs.

- The three primary tools of computer-assisted reporting are spreadsheets, database managers and online resources.

- Once learned, computer-assisted reporting permits a journalist to quickly gather and analyze comprehensive information.

- The best ways to learn the basic software tools are through trial and error, and repetition and intellectual creativity.

☞ Your Turn to Practice

1 Identify three news stories that used computer-assisted reporting to analyze government databases and won Pulitzer Prizes, and find explanations on how those stories were done.
Hint: Go to the Web site of Investigative Reporters and Editors, **www.ire.org/resourcecenter,** for each of these assignments.

2 Identify three news stories that used computer-assisted reporting on breaking news stories and on follow-up stories.

3 Find explanations on how those stories were done.

4 Find versions of database managers such as Microsoft Access and of spreadsheet software such as Microsoft Excel, and open those programs to look at their basic appearances and tools.

www
For a look at related exercises to this book, please go to **www.ire.org/carbook/chapter1**

PART **I**

Learning
Computer-Assisted
Reporting
Skills

▼

▼

▼

▼

▼

▼

▼

CHAPTER 2

Online Resources

Researching and Finding Data on the Internet

▼

> *Newsday's series revealed that doctors who have been punished for serious or even fatal wrongdoing often continue to work for managed health care companies.*
>
> *The health care companies and agencies probably never envisioned their Web sites being scrutinized in the manner reporter Thomas Maier examined them. From the board-certification site, he found doctors who erroneously claimed board certification in the Web listings of managed care companies.*
>
> **— Richard J. Dalton Jr., Newsday**

Maier's reporting, assisted by database expert Dalton, involved the use of a huge database, numerous interviews and a successful open-record lawsuit. But, as noted in the preceding quote, it also made clever use of the Internet by comparing the names of disciplined doctors with the names of doctors who were part of the managed care network.

Many journalists are used to running to a press conference, firing questions at a spokesperson, dashing back to the office, frantically making phone calls while simultaneously writing the story and then confirming a few key facts before the story is published or aired.

But in the past few years, journalists have augmented this routine by going online and electronically grabbing information from the Internet and, more specifically, the **World Wide Web,** as Maier and Dalton did. They use the Web to check facts, get story ideas, conduct interviews, add context and depth to their stories and download crucial databases. The change has been nothing short of revolutionary. (Don't forget, however, that many databases can be obtained directly from an agency on diskette, CD-ROM or computer tape.)

The fact is that computer-assisted reporting has helped to level the playing field between journalists and those on whom they report. It also has leveled the playing field between small and large news organizations. On stories involving data, a journalist with computer-assisted reporting skills and a home computer can match or exceed the work of a colleague at a larger news organization.

But along with the increased speed of the Web and the widespread availability of databases have come new and greater responsibilities. With electronic information and data, your errors can be as significant as your accomplishments. This should not scare or discourage you as a journalist from learning computer-assisted reporting, but it does mean you should proceed with some cautions.

▼ Verifying and Double-Checking

If you are going to use electronic information and data for journalism, you must be more vigilant and skeptical than ever. Electronic information distributed by a government or businesses is not necessarily more accurate or complete than information on paper. The good news, however, is that electronic information and data offer one important advantage to a journalist: Flaws can be detected more quickly than those on paper. (Chapter 9 discusses working with data.)

A journalist also needs to be more sensitive to privacy and ethical issues when working with electronic data. The speed with which data can be analyzed and cross-referenced sometimes makes a journalist rush through concerns that might cause the journalist to otherwise pause. Careless data processing may inadvertently divulge confidential or embarrassing information that is not pertinent to a story. It is incumbent on the journalist to verify whether the information has any merit.

A student in one of my classes once obtained a database of local gun permit applications with the applicants' names, the type of firearm and other information. If the applicant received the permit, there was an entry with the firearm license number. If the application was denied, the reason for the denial was indicated. Because space was limited on the form, the denial was only a few words. In several instances, the clerk had typed "mental case" as the reason for the denial.

While the reason was clearly stated, the student had a responsibility to gather more information about the denied permits before there could even be a discussion of how to, or whether to, use that reason for the denial. For example, how did the clerk determine the applicant's mental stability? What criteria were used? Did anyone review the clerk's decision? Would you reveal the applicant's name, and under what circumstances? How would you write about this? These are just some of the issues you must keep in mind as you learn these new skills.

▼ Electronic Information and Data

For the purposes of this handbook, we will define electronic information as "text." It can be e-mail, an announcement, a press release or a report. Although computer-assisted reporting is the analysis and management of datasets, you must have online skills to identify and gather information about the data.

In this chapter, we cover basic search techniques and sources of useful electronic information, but mostly we focus on databases that are in **columns** and **rows,** because that is how databases are formatted. First, however, it is important that you understand how a column and row database differs from electronic text when you are doing a search.

As journalists, we deal with text-long strings of letters and words that run from line to line to the end of the screen. When we get to the end of one screen, we keep on typing to the next screen. Everything pours out in one long scroll. But in the computer-assisted reporting world, text is often the first and last thing we use. We go to text to find out about databases, and after we have done our research and analysis on datasets, we use text to write the story.

We work with columns and rows of data because that format allows us to sort and summarize easily in what Richard Mullins, a long-time CAR practitioner, likes to call "the two-dimensional world" — that is, a world reduced to a flat screen of information.

Although many journalists are initially reluctant to use this method of looking at information on a computer screen, we're all familiar with it. We not only use phone directories and city directories, but we put columns and rows in our own work. This kind of information is also known as "tabular" because when columns and rows are combined, they are called **tables.**

In any newspaper, we find pages and pages of columns and rows, or
tabular information. You may see charts of names and numbers in the
front section about things such as taxes, census studies and budgets. In
the business section you see columns and rows listing stocks, bonds and
mutual funds. In the sports section you may see the scores of professional and college teams, as well as statistics on individual athletes.

We ponder the two-dimensional world every day. If we're interested in
sports, we check the rankings of teams. The first column in **Figure 2-1**
contains the ranking, the second the team's name and the third the
team's record. As you can see in **Figure 2-1,** the columns are categories
of information, and each row (also known as a record) has information
for each category for a particular team.

Figure 2-1

Team Rankings		
Rank	Team	Games
1	Nebraska	10-0
2	Texas	9-1
3	Florida	9-1
4	Miami	8-2

Most journalists have written lists with columns and rows by hand,
but it's easy to lose a list. If the list gets too long, it is hard to sort.
Columns and rows on paper are "petrified" information, but information recorded electronically is flexible. With software tools, you can
change the order of the columns and rows, group categories of data
and total it and can compare it with other data.

Frequently journalists need to estimate how much the salaries of public employees cost taxpayers. The information regarding people's salaries
contains three categories: name, title and salary. Each row is a record of
each person's information in those three categories (see **Figure 2-2**).

Figure 2-2

Salaries

Name	Title	Salary
Josephine Smith	Comptroller	$54,000
Juan Hinojosa	City Manager	$72,000
James Brown	Purchasing Agent	$44,000
Joan Bertrand	Parks Administrator	$48,000

Using the other two basic tools of computer-assisted reporting — the spreadsheet and the database manager — you can look at a list and sort it quickly, as you can with sports standings. In **Figure 2-3,** for example, the person with the highest salary appears first in the list.

Figure 2-3

Salaries

Name	Title	Annual Salary
Juan Hinojosa	City Manager	$72,000
Josephine Smith	Comptroller	$54,000
Joan Bertrand	Parks Administrator	$48,000
James Brown	Purchasing Agent	$44,000

Being able to organize information by category or order can be invaluable. Whether you're working with four names or thousands of rows, a spreadsheet or database manager gives you control. Using the same command, you can quickly sort from the highest at the top to the lowest at the bottom.

▼ Electronic Information and Data on the Internet

Of course, before you can do any analysis, first you have to find and obtain the data, and there are several ways to do that. You can download it from the Web, acquire it on a storage device such as a diskette or CD-ROM or build your own database.

Admittedly, finding online resources can be time-consuming, frustrating and pointless, but if you approach the Web with a plan and an understanding of what it has to offer, you will reap rich results. Overall, a journalist uses online information for several purposes, including the following.

- *Research.* A journalist can go to the Internet — the largest library in the world — by searching through news clips, academic papers, books and other documents.
- *Interviews.* Online reporting allows a journalist to widen the inquiry when searching for people such as experts, victims, witnesses and participants.
- *Database gathering.* A journalist can transfer data to his or her own computer over phone lines or networks (known as **downloading**).
- *Analysis.* When a journalist finds a database that could be useful, he or she can use spreadsheet or database manager software on the computer on which it is located to analyze that information at leisure.

In this chapter, we take a quick look at useful online information and research techniques and then concentrate on finding databases and downloading them.

▼ Using Online Resources

Although some journalists still struggle with the practical uses of online resources, for most it is second nature to consult them for daily stories and long-term projects.

As long ago as the early 1980s, reporters at American Banker and The Kansas City Star used Lexis/Nexis — a fee-based service of news articles and lawsuits — to locate and research court cases involving the con men who caused the collapse of dozens of lending institutions. Using

keywords for the perpetrators and the banks, the reporters swiftly identified the states' lending institutions that were affected.

In 1991, Mike Berens, then a journalist at The Columbus Dispatch in
Ohio, used online databases to track a multistate serial killer. By selecting and reviewing unsolved murders of women along interstates, Berens
recognized a pattern of killings.

In 1992, Dave Davis and Ted Wendling at The Plain Dealer in Cleve-
land used online resources to produce riveting stories about the perils
of radiation treatment. A Pulitzer Prize finalist, the series initially relied
on an online database of the Nuclear Regulatory Commission, called
NUDOCS. A relentless search of the two million records in NUDOCS
resulted in leads and details about people who had died from medical
overdoses of radiation.

Reporters used online resources to gather information about the
southern California earthquake in 1994 by going to geological sites and
finding people to interview through Internet discussion groups. In fact,
after phone service was cut off, the Internet kept running.

Online resources not only helped reporters with information about
the 1995 bombing of the Oklahoma City federal building, but some of
the first information about the bombing appeared in discussion groups
on the Internet. Information about militia groups and their beliefs
appeared in various newsgroups, online areas where users posted messages. News about survivors and the government's response to the
bombing appeared in online sites such as those run by the Red Cross
and the state of Oklahoma. Reporters found experts and detailed
research materials pertinent to the story online.

Newsday's Pulitzer Prize–winning coverage of the TWA Flight 800
plane crash in 1996 utilized online commercial databases, Web sites,
newsgroups (online discussion groups) and Federal Aviation Administration and National Transportation Safety Board databases and reports. In
the same year, The Times-Picayune in New Orleans subscribed to online
fishery mailing lists to track issues, locate sources and ask questions
about an oceans study. Their article won a Pulitzer Prize.

Journalists found valuable information on terrorist attacks on Web
sites run by religious and nonprofit organizations, sites that provided
blueprints of buildings, databases on airport security and air safety and
online government reports. So it's clear that the Internet can provide a
quick jump-start for any story.

What Online Resources to Use

What's out there in the online world? At first glance, it may look like
way too much. But one way to get on top of the online world is to think
of it as having two major forms: (1) traditional secondary resources, such
as the costly archives of newspapers and court records; and (2) nontradi-
tional primary resources, such as government databases and discussion
groups, which cost very little or nothing.

The next challenge is figuring out whether you can trust what you
find. Of course, "trust" is not the right word. As we said earlier, you must
verify and cross-reference whatever you find in the online world. You
need to determine which Web sites are credible and who created them.
For example, Web sites with addresses that end in ".gov" are constructed
only by government agencies and consequently are as reliable as any
other government source.

But e-mail and discussion groups are as reliable as irate citizens at an
open city council meeting or a conversation you overheard in a restaurant. As a good journalist, before you use such information, you need
to accurately identify the source, do a follow-up interview and verify
what you were told. Blindly repeating what was heard never serves a
journalist well.

Electronic Library Researchers and Journalists

Some journalists would rather let experienced and professional online
researchers do their online work for them. Electronic library researchers
(also known as **searchers**) are one of the most important resources for
the journalist heading online. Like traditional librarians, they know
where information is stored and how to find it. A searcher should serve
as a guide, provide invaluable advice and knowledge, help with complex
searches and direct the journalist to the right resources.

But journalists must learn how to go into the electronic stacks themselves so they'll know what questions to ask a searcher and how to do
some of their own research. This is the same principle as learning spreadsheets and database managers instead of relying on a data processor.

A good searcher thinks like a journalist, and a journalist can pick up
insightful reporting techniques from a searcher. Many journalists are
deft at interviewing primary resources, whether people or raw documents, but they avoid acquiring the searcher's skills to "interview"
secondary sources such as articles, papers, books or other literature.
(By interviewing documents, we mean doing research, coming up with

more questions and then doing more research to answer those questions.) With both sets of skills, a journalist can go farther by linking the library materials to interviews and picking up more tips.

Newspaper Clips and Databases

As Berens' work on a multistate serial killer showed, an electronic library search of newspaper clips can turn up patterns and story tips. There are several commercial services, such as **Lexis/Nexis,** that provide this kind of resource. Library researchers are extremely skilled at searching newspaper archives, and a good journalist never begins work on a story without first checking the archives. The service is often free for university students, but the charges are significant for private individuals and newsrooms.

The biggest advantage of searching Lexis/Nexis is the scope of the information. The disadvantage is that lengthy searches can be very expensive. However, there are many free indexes to newspapers and their archives are available before you are forced to pay for the information. One free service is Lexis-One. Two others are the collection of Special Libraries Association's News Division at **http://sunsite.unc. edu/slanews/internet/archives.html** and Alan Schlein's **www. deadlineonline.com.**

E-mail, Listservs and Newsgroups

Another resource is **e-mail,** which is now such a predominant method of communication that it needs no introduction. Many students and journalists, however, still don't appreciate how useful it can be for collecting information.

What's a more practical use? Let's say you are looking for experts on health insurance. Send a message to ProfNet, which acts as an e-mail distribution system. ProfNet, operated by PR Newswire (**www. prnewswire.com**), takes your e-mail and forwards it to experts on the subject, who reply to your query online or by phone or fax. Of course, you have to regard the experts with the same degree of skepticism as any source, but ProfNet has proven itself to be a good resource for journalists.

"Many reporters I talk to say they think using ProfNet is somehow cheating; it makes it too easy to find the right person to talk to," says Kenton Robinson, a long-time user of online resources and now a writer at The Day in New London, Connecticut. "But there is an art to the query, as it were. You must make it as precise *(and concise) as possible* and make clear how close your deadline looms."

With e-mail you also can join discussion groups including listservs and **newsgroups,** which form around specific topics. An advantage of these discussion groups is that you can ask a question of hundreds or thousands of people who belong to a **listserv** or a newsgroup. You also can search the archives of these discussion groups to read their comments.

To find a listserv for a particular topic, you can go to **www.lizst.com** and type in particular keywords, as shown in **Figure 2-4.** Since the terrorist attacks, some government or commercial Web sites consider certain information too sensitive to publish on the Web.)

Figure 2-4

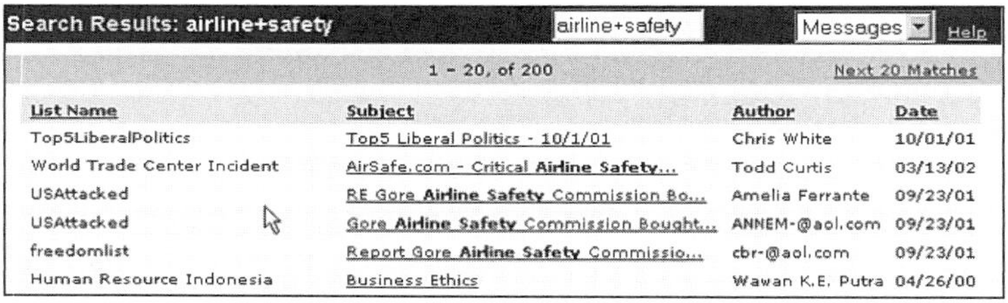
Search Results: airline+safety — airline+safety — Messages — Help

1 - 20, of 200 — Next 20 Matches

List Name	Subject	Author	Date
Top5LiberalPolitics	Top5 Liberal Politics - 10/1/01	Chris White	10/01/01
World Trade Center Incident	AirSafe.com - Critical **Airline Safety**...	Todd Curtis	03/13/02
USAttacked	RE Gore **Airline Safety** Commission Bo...	Amelia Ferrante	09/23/01
USAttacked	Gore **Airline Safety** Commission Bought...	ANNEM-@aol.com	09/23/01
freedomlist	Report Gore **Airline Safety** Commissio...	cbr-@aol.com	09/23/01
Human Resource Indonesia	Business Ethics	Wawan K.E. Putra	04/26/00

Once you've decided on the listserv you want to monitor, you join it. For example, if a journalist wants to join the listserv of the National Institute for Computer-Assisted Reporting, he or she sends a message like the one in **Figure 2-5.** The journalist's name is Helen Jenks.

Figure 2-5

To: listserv@po.lists.missouri.edu

subscribe nicar-l helen jenks

Now Helen will have access to message boards on which people discuss computer-assisted reporting. If she joins a listserv on environmental issues or military budgets, she can view messages about those topics. She can also send her own messages to the listservs, requesting help or information.

One problem with listservs is that all the mail is sent to your electronic mailbox. People do not always stick to the point, and sometimes they argue endlessly. If Helen doesn't want to receive all that mail, she can join a newsgroup on the Internet instead.

Newsgroups are like listservs, but instead of your mailbox, messages are sent to an area you can visit electronically. It's more like reading messages posted on a bulletin board. One way to join newsgroups is to go to the search engine Google (**www.google.com**) and choose "Groups" in the top menu bar. (Note that you can reach news stories, too, by clicking on "News" in the top menu.) This takes you to a list of topics you can research, as shown in **Figure 2-6.**

Figure 2-6

If you click on "sci," for example, you get a list of newsgroups related to that topic. You can see in **Figure 2-7** that this is a good way to view discussions on aircraft safety.

Figure 2-7

By choosing aeronautics (**Figure 2-8**), you can look at posts on aeronautics and air safety issues.

Figure 2-8

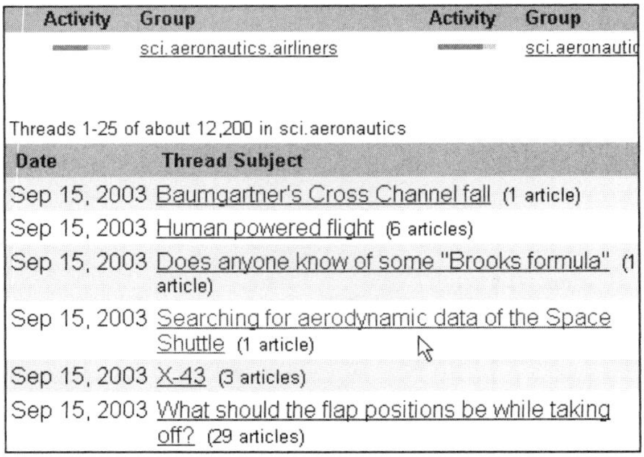

▼ Using Boolean Logic to Search the Internet

Beyond the vast prairie of e-mail lies the Internet. For many students and journalists, the Internet is like a huge ocean, or maybe a landfill. You can fish valuable objects out of it, but often you have to troll for a long time or dig so deep that it's not worth the trouble. Yet, every day new search engines and indexing tools make Internet searches much less arduous.

By clicking on words and phrases, a searcher can jump to other pages on other computers around the world. Furthermore, the Internet carries not only data and text but also sound and video.

Journalists waste a lot of time bouncing around the Web because they don't know about search methods and indexes. We will cover **Boolean logic** in more detail in later chapters, but every journalist should know the impact of three Boolean words — "and," "or" and "not" — on searches.

In a search, if you type that you want information on "dogs AND fleas," you will get information that covers only *both*. If you type that you want information on "dogs OR fleas," you will get a lot more information because your search results will include information about dogs only, about fleas only and about both dogs and fleas. If you type that you are looking for information about "dogs but NOT fleas," then you will get only information about dogs with no mention of fleas. (There probably isn't a whole lot of information there.)

Many search engines, such as Google.com or Altavista.com, automatically choose whether to use "and" or "or" without guidance from you. So, as Newsday reporter and expert searcher Tom McGinty says, always read each search engine's explanation. In **Figure 2-9,** we see Google's search tips.

Figure 2-9

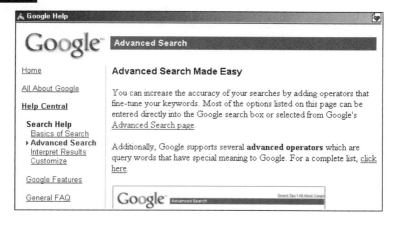

You should also know where to find good indexes for general topic searches. Index sites include Yahoo.com and the other sites mentioned earlier in the chapter. Indexes are constructed by journalists for journalists. Some of the quick-start indexes are Nettour at **www.ire.org** and The Reporter's Desktop at **www.reporter.org.** Others that are more detailed include the Resource Center of Investigative Reporters and Editors Inc. at **www.ire.org/resourcecenter** and The Poynter Institute for Media Studies at **www.poynter.org.**

Some good reference books for journalists are "Great Scouts" by Nora Paul and Margot Williams; "Find It Online" by Allan Schlein; "A Journalist's Guide to the Internet" by Chris Callahan; "The Online Journalist" by Randy Reddick and Elliot King; and "Super Searchers in the News," a book of interviews by Paula Hane.

▼ Downloading Government Databases

When doing computer-assisted reporting, an important, and easy, task is finding and downloading those free international, U.S., state and local databases — usually government related. Both Yahoo.com and a Web site called Search Systems (**www.searchsystems.net**) list all kinds of government databases available online. The U.S. government, which offers many databases on its activities and those of other countries, has gateways to its databases at **www.fedworld.gov** and **www.census.gov,** among many others.

Remember that no index is complete, but it's a valuable place to start. Recently, because of security concerns about terrorists, governments have removed some information from the Web, but this hasn't stemmed the ever-growing amount of information and data on government sites.

Databases from the Web can come in many forms, most of which can be imported with relative ease into Microsoft Excel or Microsoft Access. For example, the U.S. Bureau of the Census offers files in several formats (see **Figure 2-10**).

Figure 2-10

Exhibits:

o **Report Text**: *(PDF, 90k) (TXT, 10k)*

o **Exhibit 1:** U.S. International Trade in Goods and Services: January 2000 to Present - Imports, Exports, and Balance of Goods on a Balance of Payments Basis and Services (Seasonally Adjusted) *(PDF, 10k) (TXT, 15k) (WK4, 85k)*

o **Exhibit 2:** U.S. International Trade in Goods and Services Three-Month Moving Averages : January 2000 to Present (Seasonally Adjusted) *(PDF, 10k) (TXT, 10k) (WK4, 80k)*

o **Exhibit 3:** U.S. Services by Major Category -- Exports: January 2000 to Present (Seasonally Adjusted) *(PDF, 10k) (TXT, 10k) (WK4, 80k)*

Some of the formats of datasets, from the easiest to the most difficult, include the following.

• *Excel or database files.* These files are often listed with .xls or .dbf as the file extension name, such as salaries.xls and Contribution.dbf. You will see many examples of the actual data in the coming chapters.

- *HTML files.* These are tables that have extensions of .html and can be read and opened automatically by a spreadsheet. You can download a file or copy and paste it into a spreadsheet (see **Figure 2-11**).

Figure 2-11

Annex Table 4 Healthy life expectancy (HALE) in all Member States, estimates for 2000

| Member State | Total population at birth | Healthy life expectancy (years) | | | | | | | | Expectation of lost healthy years at birth | |
| | | Males | | | | Females | | | | | |
		At birth	Uncertainty Interval	At age 60	Uncertainty Interval	At birth	Uncertainty Interval	At age 60	Uncertainty Interval	Males	Females
Afghanistan	33.8	35.1	30.3 - 40.4	7.1	5.5 - 8.8	32.5	26.2 - 39.5	5.8	2.6 - 9.0	9.1	12.5
Albania	59.4	56.5	54.4 - 59.3	11.4	10.3 - 12.6	62.3	59.9 - 64.8	14.4	13.0 - 16.0	7.9	10.6
Algeria	58.4	58.4	55.8 - 61.9	11.1	9.4 - 13.1	58.3	54.5 - 62.2	11.0	8.9 - 12.9	9.7	12.9
Andorra	71.8	69.8	67.4 - 73.0	17.0	15.4 - 18.7	73.7	70.7 - 77.9	19.4	17.3 - 22.5	7.3	10.1
Angola	36.9	36.2	33.7 - 42.0	7.4	5.3 - 10.1	37.6	33.3 - 42.8	7.3	4.6 - 10.3	8.1	10.8
Antigua and Barbuda	61.9	61.7	58.4 - 64.8	14.8	13.5 - 16.3	62.1	59.0 - 65.2	15.4	14.1 - 16.9	10.1	14.5

- *Fixed format files.* These are in the form of evenly lined up columns, and they often have a .txt extension. Sections of data on the screen can be copied and pasted directly onto a spreadsheet. The data on world population projections from the Census Bureau is shown in **Figure 2-12.**

Figure 2-12

Total Midyear Population for the 1950-2050

Year	Population	Average annual growth rate (%)	Average annual population change
1950	2,555,360,972	1.47	37,785,986
1951	2,593,146,958	1.61	42,060,389
1952	2,635,207,347	1.71	45,337,232
1953	2,680,544,579	1.77	47,971,823
1954	2,728,516,402	1.87	51,451,629
1955	2,779,968,031	1.89	52,959,308
1956	2,832,927,339	1.95	55,827,050
1957	2,888,754,389	1.94	56,506,563
1958	2,945,260,952	1.76	52,335,100
1959	2,997,596,052	1.39	42,073,278
1960	3,039,669,330	1.33	40,792,172
1961	3,080,461,502	1.80	56,094,590

- *Delimited files.* These have marks — commas, semicolons, tabs — between each column of information and often have .csv extensions. Spreadsheets and database managers can open the file easily. **Figure 2-13** shows an example of state population data.

Figure 2-13

```
Georgia,"7,201","7,875","8,413","9,200","9,869"
Hawaii,"1,187","1,257","1,342","1,553","1,812"
Idaho,"1,163","1,347","1,480","1,622","1,739"
Illinois,"11,830","12,051","12,266","12,808","13,440"
Indiana,"5,803","6,045","6,215","6,404","6,546"
Iowa,"2,842","2,900","2,941","2,994","3,040"
Kansas,"2,565","2,668","2,761","2,939","3,108"
Kentucky,"3,860","3,995","4,098","4,231","4,314"
Louisiana,"4,342","4,425","4,535","4,840","5,133"
Maine,"1,241","1,259","1,285","1,362","1,423"
Maryland,"5,042","5,275","5,467","5,862","6,274"
```

- *Portable document files or PDF files.* These files are made for printouts and are not for data analysis. They are the bane of computer-assisted reporting. While they may look like other data, as in **Figure 2-13,** they require special procedures or software to import them into spreadsheets or database managers (see **Figure 2-14**).

Figure 2-14

4

Part A: Seasonally Adjusted

Exhibit 1. U. S. International Trade in Goods and

In millions of dollars. Details may not equal totals due to seasonal adjustment and

Period	Balance			Exports		
	Total	Goods (1)	Services	Total	Goods (1)	Services
2000						
Jan.- Dec.	-378,681	-452,423	73,742	1,064,239	771,994	292,245
Jan.- Aug.	-242,540	-293,887	51,347	702,627	508,416	194,211
January	-26,637	-33,217	6,580	84,704	61,256	23,448
February	-29,299	-35,727	6,428	84,934	60,939	23,995
March	-31,237	-37,511	6,274	86,456	62,290	24,166
April	-29,101	-36,391	7,290	86,061	63,147	24,914

▼ Downloading Different Files

Let's do five kinds of downloads and open some of them in Excel. The first is from the World Health Organization's statistics site (**http://www3.who.int/whosis/menu.cfm**) of an Excel worksheet of Healthy Life Expectancy in certain countries. This is an easier way to download the same information in **Figure 2-11. Figure 2-15** shows the site that allows you to download the data.

Figure 2-15

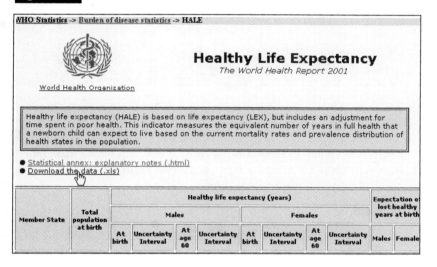

When you click on the file, it automatically downloads into Excel, as shown in **Figure 2-16.** Once you save it to a folder on your computer, you can begin your analysis. (Although in this case, it may not be necessary, always check for viruses whenever you download files.)

Figure 2-16

	A	B	C	D	E	F	G
1	**Annex Table 4 Healthy life expectancy (HALE) in all Member States, estimate**						
2	These figures were produced by WHO using the best available evidence. They are not necessarily the official statistics						
3	LEVEL						
4							Healthy life
5			Total population			Males 2001	
6		Member State	At birth 2000	At birth 2001	At birth	Uncertainty interval	At age 60
7							
8	1 Afghanistan		33.8	33.4	31.1	24.9 - 37.6	4.9
9	2 Albania		58.6	58.7	55.9	55.0 - 58.4	8.8
10	3 Algeria		57.5	57.8	55.8	54.2 - 58.5	10.3
11	4 Andorra		70.8	70.9	68.8	67.9 - 70.3	15.8
12	5 Angola		28.9	28.7	25.7	19.8 - 31.9	5.8
13	6 Antigua and Barbuda		59.7	59.7	56.9	55.4 - 60.0	10.3
14	7 Argentina		62.9	63.1	60.6	59.6 - 62.2	11.9
15	8 Armenia		57.9	58.3	55.4	54.1 - 57.3	9.2
16	9 Australia		71.4	71.6	70.1	69.4 - 71.2	16.4
17	10 Austria		70.7	71.0	68.9	68.5 - 69.7	15.7

◄ ◄ ► ►► \ Annex Table 4 final /

Now let's try an HTML file. In this example, we will copy and paste the desired database from a Web site that keeps track of organ transplants. When you go to **www.unos.org,** you will find tables with data on deaths of people waiting for transplants (see **Figure 2-17**).

Figure 2-17

UNOS   About UNOS   Newsroom   Patients   Data   Resources   Links   You Can Help!   Search

_Critical Data
Waiting List
Donors
Transplants
Milestones
Return Home

Total	55990	17623	1335	2581	195	3968	203	3855

Reported Deaths on the Waiting List By Organ and Year of Removal or Death:
1992-2001 as of May 24, 2002 (Updated Annually)

Organ	Year										Total
	1992	1993	1994	1995	1996	1997	1998	1999	2000	2001	
	#	#	#	#	#	#	#	#	#	#	#
Heart	776	763	730	772	747	782	769	721	601	622	7,283
Heart-Lung	45	51	47	28	52	57	43	53	43	40	459
Intestine	0	4	14	19	22	42	45	43	22	43	254
Kidney	1,079	1,321	1,390	1,538	1,853	2,054	2,424	3,219	2,918	2,861	20657
Kidney-Pancreas	15	61	71	87	91	124	97	171	193	214	1,124
Liver	530	592	685	831	998	1,187	1,421	1,824	1,758	1,975	11801
Lung	229	254	290	344	395	419	505	588	487	477	3,988
Pancreas	35	3	13	4	4	13	14	19	15	36	156
Total	2,654	2,975	3,126	3,498	4,008	4,466	5,125	6,387	5,925	6,124	44288

Note: Date of death on the waiting list has been collected since the launch of UNET on 10/25/99. Prior to that date, only the date of waiting list removal was collected.

Highlight the table you want and then click on "Copy" in the Menu Bar, as shown in **Figure 2-18.**

Figure 2-18

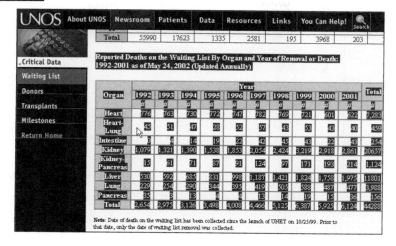

Open Excel and click on the top box (A1) of the grid. Then go to the Menu Bar and click on "Edit" and then "Paste," and the data on the deaths are as in **Figure 2-19.**

Figure 2-19

	C	D	E	F	G	H	I	J	K	L
1	Waiting List By Organ and Year of Removal or Death: 1992-2001 as of May 24, 2002 (Updated Annually)									
2										
3				Year						
4	1993	1994	1995	1996	1997	1998	1999	2000	2001	Total
5	#	#	#	#	#	#	#	#	#	#
6	763	730	772	747	782	769	721	601	622	7,28
7	51	47	28	52	57	43	53	43	40	45
8	4	14	19	22	42	45	43	22	43	25
9	1,321	1,390	1,538	1,853	2,054	2,424	3,219	2,918	2,861	2065
10	61	71	87	91	124	97	171	193	214	1,12
11	592	685	831	998	1,187	1,421	1,824	1,758	1,975	1180
12	254	290	344	395	419	505	588	487	477	3,98
13	3	13	4	4	13	14	19	15	36	15
14	2,975	3,126	3,498	4,008	4,466	5,125	6,387	5,925	6,124	4428

Now we will get a fixed format file from the Web. Go to the Census Web site, **www.census.gov,** and click through on Foreign Trade. You will come to the page where you can download reports. Pick Exhibit 1

for information on the balance of payments and click on TXT (see
Figure 2-20).

Figure 2-20

Highlights:

o U.S. International Trade in Goods and Services - Highlights

Exhibits:

o **Report Text**: *(PDF, 90k)* *(TXT, 10k)*

o **Exhibit 1:** U.S. International Trade in Goods and Services: January
  2000 to Present - Imports, Exports, and Balance of Goods on a
  Balance of Payments Basis and Services (Seasonally Adjusted)
  (PDF, 10k) *(TXT, 15k)* *(WK4, 85k)*

o **Exhibit 2:** U.S. International Trade in Goods and Services Three-
  Month Moving Averages : January 2000 to Present (Seasonally
  Adjusted) *(PDF, 10k)* *(TXT, 10k)* *(WK4, 80k)*

o **Exhibit 3:** U.S. Services by Major Category -- Exports: January
  2000 to Present (Seasonally Adjusted) *(PDF, 10k)* *(TXT, 10k)*
  (WK4, 80k)

When you click on TXT, you get a fixed format table, meaning all the
columns are justified left or right, as shown in **Figure 2-21.**

Figure 2-21

```
PART A: SEASONALLY ADJUSTED

EXHIBIT 1. U.S. INTERNATIONAL TRADE IN GOODS AND SERVICES
           JANUARY 2000 TO AUGUST 2002

(In millions of dollars. Details may not equal totals due to seasonal
adjustment and rounding.  (R) Revised.)


                                        Balance

        Period           Total        Goods (1)        Services


2000

Jan.- Dec.              -378,681       -452,423          73,742
Jan.- Aug.             -242,540       -293,887          51,347
January                -26,637        -33,217           6,580
February               -29,299        -35,727           6,428
March                  -31,237        -37,511           6,274
April                  -29,101        -36,391           7,290
May                    -31,070        -37,476           6,406
```

This time we will save the table directly to our computer hard drive. Go to "File" on the Menu Bar and click on "Save As," as shown in **Figure 2-22.**

Figure 2-22

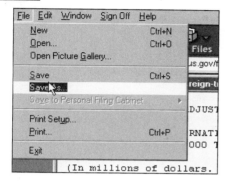

We will save this as a text file because it is in the fixed format, as shown in **Figure 2-23.**

Figure 2-23

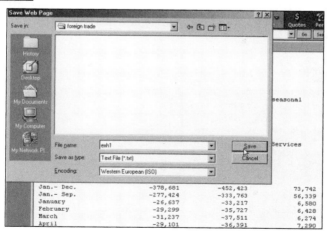

Now comes the tricky part: We will try to open this file with Excel. Click on "Open" under "File," and you will see the Wizard screen shown in **Figure 2-24.** The Wizard notes whether the text is in fixed format or has a delimiter. It also allows you to choose the row with which to import, meaning that you can get rid of the sentences across the top and start with the titles of the columns. In this case, we choose row 10.

Figure 2-24

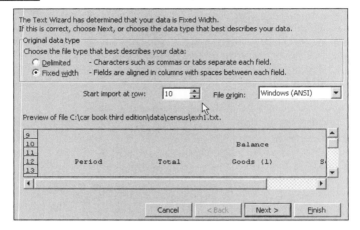

Now click on "Next," and you will get a screen where the Wizard has drawn lines between the columns. Notice that you can create, move or delete the lines. In this case, the Wizard guessed correctly, as shown in **Figure 2-25.**

Figure 2-25

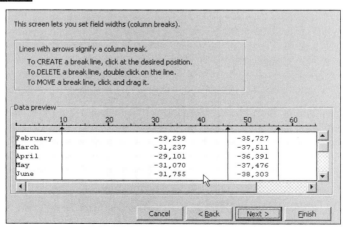

Hit "Next" again, and the Wizard now offers the option to change "Data Types," as shown in **Figure 2-26.** In this case, we will use what it suggests. (We will talk about data types in later chapters.)

Figure 2-26

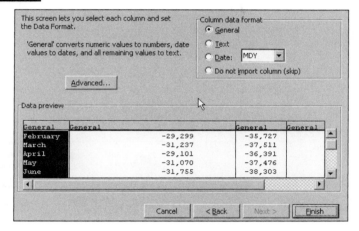

Click on "Finish," and the data in the worksheet is now ready for analysis. However, you should immediately save this as an Excel file, as shown in **Figure 2-27.**

Figure 2-27

	A	B	C	D	E
6					
7	2000				
8					
9	Jan.- Dec.	-378,681	-452,423	73,742	
10	Jan.- Aug.	-242,540	-293,887	51,347	
11	January	-26,637	-33,217	6,580	
12	February	-29,299	-35,727	6,428	
13	March	-31,237	-37,511	6,274	
14	April	-29,101	-36,391	7,290	
15	May	-31,070	-37,476	6,406	
16	June	-31,755	-38,303	6,548	
17					
18	July	-32,453	-38,393	5,940	
19	August	-30,988	-36,869	5,881	
20	September	-34,884	-39,876	4,992	
21	October	-34,281	-40,206	5,925	
22	November	-33,054	-38,786	5,732	

Next we download a delimited file of the same information. The file looks like this in the Wizard screen when we try to open it in Excel. Note that the Wizard sees a delimited file, shown in **Figure 2-28.**

Figure 2-28

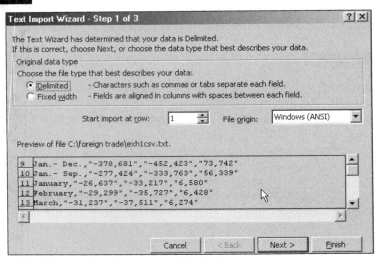

Click on "Next" and check what the Wizard identifies as the "delimiter" — in this case, a comma. (You will also need to click on "Tab" to blank out that box.) See **Figure 2-29.**

Figure 2-29

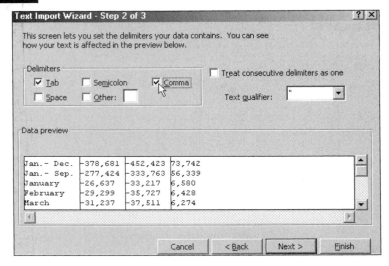

From here, it is the same as the fixed format. Click on "Next," and the Wizard offers "Data Types" again. Click on "Finish," and your data are again in Excel where you can work with it.

▼ Using File Transfer Protocol

Another way to download information is by a technique called **file transfer protocol,** also known as "ftp-ing." Many Web sites, including those of the Census Bureau and NICAR, allow you to do this, especially for larger files.

To download this way, go to the file transfer protocol site, which sometimes has a site **address** different from most Web sites and sometimes starts with ftp. In NICAR's case, it is **ftp.nicar.org.** When you go to an ftp site, you will see **folders** (known as directories). Let's use the Census site for loading detailed information about a state (see **Figure 2-30**). When you click on particular files, you start a download.

Figure 2-30

Summary File 3 includes 484 population tables and 329 housing tables that are identified according to ge

  o **Population (P)** and **Housing (H)** tables are available to the block group
  o **Population (PCT)** and **Housing (HCT)** tables are available to the census tract level only

Data:	Access to all tables and maps in American FactFinder
Purchase Products:	Summary Files for sale through Customer Services Center
FTP Download:	All Files FTP Read me (MSWord | WordPerfect | Text)
Documentation:	Technical Documentation [PDF] (6M)

If you click on "All Files," you will be taken to an index of directories and files, shown in **Figure 2-31.** Click on a particular file, and it will start downloading. Often the files indicate their size in megabytes. This file is 1.2 megabytes or as much data as a diskette could contain.

Figure 2-31

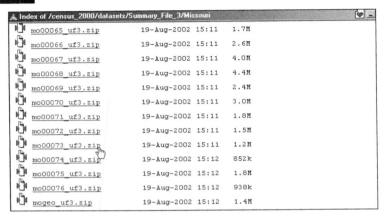

You will then be asked what you want to do with the file. Highlight that you want to save the file to disk, and click on "OK," as shown in **Figure 2-32.**

Figure 2-32

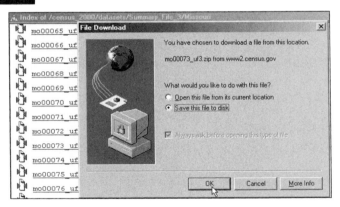

You then decide what folder to save it to, as shown in **Figure 2-33.**

Figure 2-33

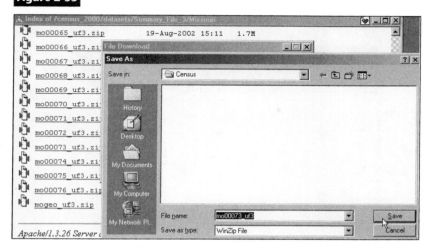

▼ Dealing with Compressed Files

You may have noticed that the downloaded file was "compressed." Many large files come in a compressed, or **zipped,** format, and you need software such as WinZip to open them, although some files "unzip" themselves. They are zipped so that they can be transferred across a network more quickly. (Mac computers have similar software called StuffIT. Many government files, however, come in PC-compatible formats, which can be difficult for a Mac to deal with.) A zipped file will have the extension ".zip."

As journalists get more databases online and from diskettes, they run into compressed files. To compress files, you run a program that squeezes the data bits together and takes the "air," or empty space, out of the information. A good compression program can sometimes reduce a three-megabyte file to half a megabyte or less, depending on the data. But you can't use that data unless you decompress it.

We'll take a brief look at WinZip, but if you're lucky, a government agency will give you a self-extracting file that automatically unzips (or expands) itself. Using WinZip, first "Open" the Archive containing the compressed file, as shown in **Figure 2-34.**

Figure 2-34

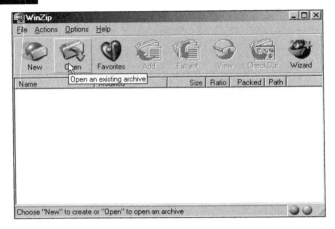

After opening it, we can see that there is one text file there, shown in **Figure 2-35.** (If we had read the information on the Census Web site, we would already know that the file is "a comma-delimited" file.)

Figure 2-35

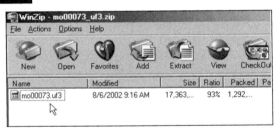

To make the file usable, you must "Extract" it, as shown in **Figure 2-36.**

Figure 2-36

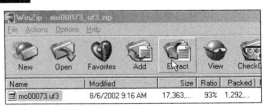

The program will want to know what folder you want to "Extract" it to, so we choose "Census" to keep all your data on Census together (see **Figure 2-37**), and the uncompressed file will be there as a text file.

Figure 2-37

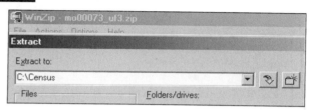

If you try to use the file in Excel, the Wizard will appear, and you will begin importing the data, just as we did earlier in the chapter (see **Figure 2-38**).

Figure 2-38

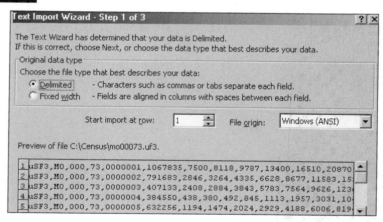

There is always the potential for problems when downloading databases. Sometimes the delimiter is misidentified, or sometimes there are hidden marks or characters in the data. But if you go slowly and make sure to examine the data closely, you can usually figure out the problem yourself. Once you do that, you are ready to do data analysis in pursuit of that good story.

▼ CAR Wars

▼ The Arkansas Democrat-Gazette embarked on a detailed look at
nonprofit, private foundations in Arkansas and found an astound-
▼ ing number. Arkansas' 273 private foundations controlled about
$1.5 billion in assets and handed out $116 million in one year. And
▼ that's for a state that lags economically behind the rest of the
nation. Without the foundations, the impoverished Mississippi River
▼ Delta would be even more desperate.

To understand the foundations' impact, we followed the money
and got the 990-PF forms that foundations have to file with the
Internal Revenue Service and got electronic data from the National
Center for Charitable Statistics. But the information goes further.
Going online from a desktop computer, we found a large collection
of Web sites devoted to the nonprofit world in general and foundations in particular. One information gold mine was the Foundation
Center in New York. The organization's Web site and its publications were invaluable.

At the Foundation Center's Web site, you can find a foundation's
records on gift recipients, foundation officers and more.

The IRS itself has a plethora of nonprofit-related information
online, including data files listing all nonprofits. The nonprofit
organization Guidestar (**www.guidestar.org**) collects and posts
the information submitted by most nonprofits to the IRS.

Our first story included key statistics on the overall picture of
foundations. Our second story focused on the details of the foundation money flowing into the Delta. Our third story looked at the
impact of the Walton Family Foundation.

Jeff Porter, formerly of the Arkansas Democrat-Gazette, now
data library director at the National Institute for Computer-Assisted
Reporting

Chapter Checklist

- The Internet can be used for several purposes including contacts, research and databases.

- Listservs and newsgroups are discussion groups on specific topics.

- Begin every story by checking electronic archives.

- Web site indexes are efficient ways to get started on research.

- Many government Web sites have data that can be downloaded for analysis.

- There are several kinds of database formats, all of which can be imported into spreadsheets and database managers with varying difficulty.

- Many times you will have to uncompress files.

 Your Turn to Practice

1 Find three federal government Web sites and three state Web sites that have data.

2 Download data from each of those sites.

3 Import the data into a spreadsheet.

Also

4 Find a listserv having to do with journalism and join it.

5 Find a newsgroup on a safety issue and read through the latest postings.

www

For more exercises in downloading and importing, go to
www.ire.org/carbook/chapter2

CHAPTER 3

Spreadsheets, Part 1

Basic Math for Journalists

> *Members of the Virginia General Assembly last year received more than $117,700 in gifts from businesses, special interest groups and lobbyists, according to computer-assisted research by Virginia Commonwealth University's Legislative Reporting class. The gifts included hunting trips to Georgia, Texas and even Canada: Two senators hunted caribou in the Arctic Circle, courtesy of the Virginia Sheriffs' Association. The most generous benefactor was Philip Morris, which treated lawmakers to almost $26,000 in meals, entertainment, golf equipment and other freebies. In January, legislators filed reports listing the gifts they received in 2000. After creating a database from the reports, VCU students identified the biggest givers and recipients of gifts — and for the first time put the database online so that the public can search it.*
>
> **— Jeff South, Virginia Commonwealth University**

This story was written from research by students in a college reporting class taught by Jeff South, a former reporter and current professor. It outdistanced work by professional journalists and received wide attention in the state of Virginia. It also showed how putting information into a **spreadsheet** for analysis can lead to powerful stories.

South's class collected information on the gifts, entered the 1,000 or so records in a spreadsheet and did simple calculations to determine who was giving gifts to legislators. The resulting stories shed new light on the legislators and those who court them.

Journalists now use spreadsheets daily, whether it is picking out patterns of waste and abuse in government or providing context for figures that show years of data and trends. The spreadsheet is particularly attractive to journalists who are just beginning to do computer-assisted reporting because it's easy to get data into a spreadsheet format.

As noted in the previous chapter, many government agencies — especially the U.S. Bureau of the Census — routinely place data files in spreadsheet format so that it can be smoothly downloaded and analyzed.

It is equally easy to enter data in a spreadsheet from documents when no electronic data exists, as the Virginia Commonwealth University students showed. The Times Picayune in New Orleans, for example, entered information on riverboat pilots from their job applications and résumés to reveal the nepotism, lack of education and criminal backgrounds among the pilots. In another instance, USA Today built a spreadsheet with information from lawsuits to show the abuse and near-enslavement of immigrants.

▼ Becoming Friendly with Numbers

Journalists constantly report on numbers, although you'll often hear them say they hated math in school — and that they *still* hate it. But many people hate flying on airplanes, but they do it because their jobs require them to. Not many of these people become pilots, but they know the plane will take them where they need to go.

The same idea applies to modern journalists and spreadsheets. A modern journalist doesn't have to be a mathematician to deal with numbers, but he or she should be willing to use a spreadsheet to get the job done. It is startling, however, how many reporters still strain for hours with pencil and paper or a calculator while trying to figure out whether the mayor has given his cronies the largest raises.

Eric Lipton, a Pulitzer Prize–winning reporter who now works for The New York Times, discovered the efficiency of spreadsheets while working at The Hartford Courant. Lipton was examining a generous early retirement plan for city employees. He was trying to calculate the **percentage** of each person's pension as compared to his or her salary at the time of retirement. Experts told him the figure should be approximately 67 percent, but in the city's early retirement plan some retirees' pensions came close to the full amount of their former salaries.

Lipton was tediously tapping a calculator for each comparison when he remembered that he had seen a spreadsheet demonstration in which the calculations were done much more rapidly. With a little help, he imported the information into a spreadsheet and learned how to do one calculation. Then he copied that calculation for more than a hundred other entries. Those calculations served as the starting point for a front-page story.

What Lipton discovered is that a spreadsheet saves an enormous amount of time, prevents unnecessary repetition and improves accuracy in calculations.

A spreadsheet allows you to quickly figure out such things as who got the most money, who got the highest percentage raise, who made the most drug arrests or which city's housing prices increased the most.

Let's look at how a spreadsheet can be used for examining pay raises. You know this year's average raise for city employees is 5 percent. At the same time, you have a list of the mayor's political appointments. (All names in this example are fictional.) Journalists often line up information like this on paper. (If you don't do it, a graphics department will make you do it.) **Figure 3-1** shows a partial list of the mayor's cronies on the city payroll.

Figure 3-1

Crony	Last year	This year
Dee Dale	45000	52000
Ed Powell	25000	30000
Jane Deed	14000	19000
Joe Smith	30000	39000
Julia Jones	50000	58000
Mark Forest	15000	21000
Mary Hill	22000	29000
Tom Brown	40000	47000

If you added dollar signs, commas and gridlines, which make it easier to keep track of the numbers, the information might look like that shown in **Figure 3-2.**

Figure 3-2

Name	Last year	This year
Dee Dale	$ 45,000.00	$ 52,000.00
Ed Powell	$ 25,000.00	$ 30,000.00
Jane Deed	$ 14,000.00	$ 19,000.00
Joe Smith	$ 30,000.00	$ 39,000.00
Julia Jones	$ 50,000.00	$ 58,000.00
Mark Forest	$ 15,000.00	$ 21,000.00
Mary Hill	$ 22,000.00	$ 29,000.00
Tom Brown	$ 40,000.00	$ 47,000.00

A spreadsheet takes this idea a step further. When a spreadsheet takes in information, it puts it in the kind of grid shown in **Figure 3-3.**

Figure 3-3

	A	B	C
1	Name	Last year	This year
2	Dee Dale	$ 45,000.00	$ 52,000.00
3	Ed Powell	$ 25,000.00	$ 30,000.00
4	Jane Deed	$ 14,000.00	$ 19,000.00
5	Joe Smith	$ 30,000.00	$ 39,000.00
6	Julia Jones	$ 50,000.00	$ 58,000.00
7	Mark Forest	$ 15,000.00	$ 21,000.00
8	Mary Hill	$ 22,000.00	$ 29,000.00
9	Tom Brown	$ 40,000.00	$ 47,000.00

As you can see, the only major change in **Figure 3-3** is that the columns are labeled with letters and the rows with numbers. This is the key concept of a spreadsheet, and it's one that you've used in other areas of life.

▼ Learning Addresses

If you have ever looked for a town on a road atlas, you've turned first to the index. The index may refer you to page 7 and to the town's location at "D4." You go to page 7. The map is laid out on a grid with letters across the top and numbers down the sides. You look down column D and then look across on row 4 to find the town.

Or perhaps you've played chess and want to replay the game. The instructions for the location of the pieces are also given with letters and numbers defining the squares. A knight, for example, will move from B1 to C3. Better yet, you may have played the game of Battleship. In that game, you make a grid with letters and numbers. You block out two or three consecutive squares for a battleship and place mines in individual squares. Your opponent does the same. Then you take turns, saying such things as "A4" or "B5." Your opponent says "hit" if your opponent's battleship is on that square, "miss" if you hit nothing, and "boom" if you hit a mine.

Spreadsheets treat your information as though it's part of a game of Battleship. Spreadsheets generally see the salary not only as $25,000, but also as "B4."

So, now we go back to the raises. You look at the first row of Dee Dale. Dale's salary increased from $45,000 to $52,000. The difference isn't too hard to see: It's $7,000. The changes in others' salaries wouldn't be hard to calculate, although if the mayor had 100 cronies, it would start to get taxing (so to speak).

An old-fashioned journalist normally analyzes raises by taking a calculator and subtracting the information in column B from that in column C. It doesn't take too long to do the calculations for a list of 10 or 20 names, but frequently a journalist is handed a list of hundreds or thousands of names. In Lipton's study of pensions and salaries, he had more than 100 names, and he was not looking ahead happily to hours of work.

This is where a spreadsheet comes in handy. In a spreadsheet, you would not subtract 45,000 from 52,000. (Remember, this is like Battleship.) You would subtract B3 from C3, but where would you put it? Well, there's a blank space next to C3, called D3. So here's the way to do it in a spreadsheet. As shown in **Figure 3-4,** you move the cursor to box D3 and click on your mouse. Then you type "=C3-B3." You type the "=" sign first so that the spreadsheet knows a formula is coming.

Figure 3-4

SUM	▼	✗ ✓ =	=C3-B3	
	A	B	C	D
1	Name	Last year	This year	
2				
3	Dee Dale	$ 45,000	$ 52,000	=C3-B3
4	Ed Powell	$ 25,000	$ 30,000	
5	Jane Deed	$ 14,000	$ 19,000	
6	Joe Smith	$ 30,000	$ 39,000	
7	Julia Jones	$ 50,000	$ 58,000	
8	Mark Forest	$ 15,000	$ 21,000	
9	Mary Hill	$ 22,000	$ 29,000	
10	Tom Brown	$ 40,000	$ 47,000	

Then you hit the "Enter" key, and you can see the result in **Figure 3-5:** $7,000.

Figure 3-5

D3	▼	=	=C3-B3	
	A	B	C	D
1	Name	Last year	This year	
2				
3	Dee Dale	$ 45,000	$ 52,000	$ 7,000
4	Ed Powell	$ 25,000	$ 30,000	
5	Jane Deed	$ 14,000	$ 19,000	
6	Joe Smith	$ 30,000	$ 39,000	
7	Julia Jones	$ 50,000	$ 58,000	
8	Mark Forest	$ 15,000	$ 21,000	
9	Mary Hill	$ 22,000	$ 29,000	
10	Tom Brown	$ 40,000	$ 47,000	

What you have done is set up a formula — not a complicated one, but a formula nonetheless — that does the simple arithmetic for you.

Now you're ready to use the spreadsheet to save time. You want to repeat the formula for every raise, but you do that not by copying $7,000 but "=C3-B3." In most spreadsheets, one way to do this is to highlight the formula by placing the cursor there and clicking on the formula. You then move the cursor to the lower right-hand corner of D3 until you see a narrow cross, as in **Figure 3-6.**

Figure 3-6

D3	▼	=	=C3-B3	
	A	B	C	D
1	Name	Last year	This year	
2				
3	Dee Dale	$ 45,000	$ 52,000	$ 7,000
4	Ed Powell	$ 25,000	$ 30,000	
5	Jane Deed	$ 14,000	$ 19,000	
6	Joe Smith	$ 30,000	$ 39,000	
7	Julia Jones	$ 50,000	$ 58,000	
8	Mark Forest	$ 15,000	$ 21,000	
9	Mary Hill	$ 22,000	$ 29,000	
10	Tom Brown	$ 40,000	$ 47,000	
11				

Next, define or shade the area you want to copy to by clicking on D3, holding down the button on your mouse, and dragging the shading to the last row in **Figure 3-7.**

Figure 3-7

	A	B	C	D
1	Name	Last year	This year	
2				
3	Dee Dale	$ 45,000	$ 52,000	$ 7,000
4	Ed Powell	$ 25,000	$ 30,000	
5	Jane Deed	$ 14,000	$ 19,000	
6	Joe Smith	$ 30,000	$ 39,000	
7	Julia Jones	$ 50,000	$ 58,000	
8	Mark Forest	$ 15,000	$ 21,000	
9	Mary Hill	$ 22,000	$ 29,000	
10	Tom Brown	$ 40,000	$ 47,000	
11				

Notice that the top line above the information in **Figure 3-6** shows that the spreadsheet does not see $7,000 in D3 but sees "=C3-B3" instead. Now let go of the clicker on your mouse, and there are all your numbers (see **Figure 3-8**).

Figure 3-8

	D3	▼	=	=C3-B3	
	A	B	C	D	
1	Name	Last year	This year		
2					
3	Dee Dale	$ 45,000	$ 52,000	$ 7,000	
4	Ed Powell	$ 25,000	$ 30,000	$ 5,000	
5	Jane Deed	$ 14,000	$ 19,000	$ 5,000	
6	Joe Smith	$ 30,000	$ 39,000	$ 9,000	
7	Julia Jones	$ 50,000	$ 58,000	$ 8,000	
8	Mark Forest	$ 15,000	$ 21,000	$ 6,000	
9	Mary Hill	$ 22,000	$ 29,000	$ 7,000	
10	Tom Brown	$ 40,000	$ 47,000	$ 7,000	
11					

What you are doing is telling the spreadsheet to do the same thing it did in D3 for the rest of the rows. As we said, the spreadsheet isn't going to copy $7,000 to every box in the D column. It's going to copy the formula of subtracting the B column from the C column in each row. Always take a close look at the column after you have copied the formula. (We will label new columns later in this chapter.) Some spreadsheets allow you to copy formulas more easily and sometimes "guess" incorrectly at what formula you want to copy. Furthermore, if you did your formula incorrectly, you will increase your error by however many rows to which you copy the formula.

So it subtracts B4 from C4, B5 from C5, and so on. Another way to copy your formula — if there are no blank rows — is to double-click once you see the narrow cross, as shown in **Figure 3-9.** When you double-click, the formula will be copied and the numbers appear until there is a blank row.

Figure 3-9

	D3	▼	=	=C3-B3	
	A	B	C	D	
1	Name	Last year	This year		
2					
3	Dee Dale	$ 45,000	$ 52,000	$ 7,000	
4	Ed Powell	$ 25,000	$ 30,000		
5	Jane Deed	$ 14,000	$ 19,000		
6	Joe Smith	$ 30,000	$ 39,000		
7	Julia Jones	$ 50,000	$ 58,000		
8	Mark Forest	$ 15,000	$ 21,000		
9	Mary Hill	$ 22,000	$ 29,000		
10	Tom Brown	$ 40,000	$ 47,000		

▼ Calculating Percentages

Let's continue our analysis of the increases. When you look at the salary increases, the largest increase is not necessarily the most important. After all, $5,000 added to $60,000 doesn't have the same impact as $5,000 added to $30,000. Often, you want to know who got the highest percentage increase. This brings you to a bugaboo of many journalists: the **percentage difference.**

Calculating a percentage difference is straightforward if you break it down into its components. If one of the mayor's cronies is making $30,000 and gets a raise to $39,000, the difference is $9,000. In this example, the percentage difference is the increase ($9,000) over the original salary: $9,000/$30,000. That means you divide 9,000 by 30,000, which gives you .30, or 30 percent.

If you were speaking it instead of calculating it, you would say, "Subtract the first column from the second column and divide the result by the first column. So in this case, it's $39,000 minus $30,000 and then $9,000 divided by $30,000." Another way to remember it is what journalist Sarah Cohen calls "NOO," which stands for (New – Old)/Old.

How would this look in a spreadsheet? You go to your spreadsheet and find the difference: $9,000, which is in box D3. The old salary is in box B3. So your formula is =D3/B3, as shown in **Figure 3-10.**

Figure 3-10

	A	B	C	D	E
	SUM	▼ ✗ ✓ =	=D3/B3		
1	Name	Last year	This year		
2					
3	Dee Dale	$ 45,000	$ 52,000	$ 7,000	=D3/B3
4	Ed Powell	$ 25,000	$ 30,000	$ 5,000	
5	Jane Deed	$ 14,000	$ 19,000	$ 5,000	
6	Joe Smith	$ 30,000	$ 39,000	$ 9,000	
7	Julia Jones	$ 50,000	$ 58,000	$ 8,000	
8	Mark Forest	$ 15,000	$ 21,000	$ 6,000	
9	Mary Hill	$ 22,000	$ 29,000	$ 7,000	
10	Tom Brown	$ 40,000	$ 47,000	$ 7,000	

Once again, you tip off the spreadsheet with the "=" sign in box E3, type "D3/B3," hit "Enter" and the result appears as shown in **Figure 3-11.**

Figure 3-11

E3	▼	**=** =D3/B3		

	A	B	C	D	E
1	Name	Last year	This year		
2					
3	Dee Dale	$ 45,000	$ 52,000	$ 7,000	0.155556
4	Ed Powell	$ 25,000	$ 30,000	$ 5,000	
5	Jane Deed	$ 14,000	$ 19,000	$ 5,000	
6	Joe Smith	$ 30,000	$ 39,000	$ 9,000	
7	Julia Jones	$ 50,000	$ 58,000	$ 8,000	
8	Mark Forest	$ 15,000	$ 21,000	$ 6,000	
9	Mary Hill	$ 22,000	$ 29,000	$ 7,000	
10	Tom Brown	$ 40,000	$ 47,000	$ 7,000	

Again, to save time, you copy the formula using the narrow cross. Your result will look like what's in **Figure 3-12**.

Figure 3-12

	A	B	C	D	E
1	Name	Last year	This year		
2					
3	Dee Dale	$ 45,000	$ 52,000	$ 7,000	0.155556
4	Ed Powell	$ 25,000	$ 30,000	$ 5,000	0.2
5	Jane Deed	$ 14,000	$ 19,000	$ 5,000	0.357143
6	Joe Smith	$ 30,000	$ 39,000	$ 9,000	0.3
7	Julia Jones	$ 50,000	$ 58,000	$ 8,000	0.16
8	Mark Forest	$ 15,000	$ 21,000	$ 6,000	0.4
9	Mary Hill	$ 22,000	$ 29,000	$ 7,000	0.318182
10	Tom Brown	$ 40,000	$ 47,000	$ 7,000	0.175

But there are too many numbers to the right of the decimal, and it looks confusing. You would never print or broadcast percentages in this form, so you use a handy icon from the spreadsheet. You highlight the column by clicking on the letter E above the top row, move the cursor onto the "%" sign, and click on it, as shown in **Figure 3-13**. (At this point, let's put column labels on the Change column and Percent column, too.)

Figure 3-13

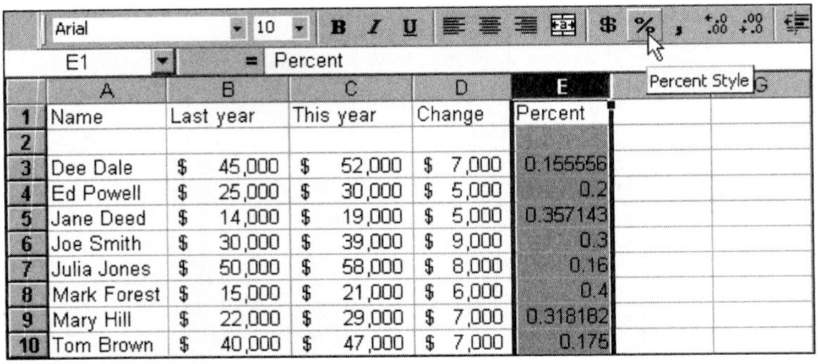

	A	B	C	D	E
1	Name	Last year	This year	Change	Percent
2					
3	Dee Dale	$ 45,000	$ 52,000	$ 7,000	0.155556
4	Ed Powell	$ 25,000	$ 30,000	$ 5,000	0.2
5	Jane Deed	$ 14,000	$ 19,000	$ 5,000	0.357143
6	Joe Smith	$ 30,000	$ 39,000	$ 9,000	0.3
7	Julia Jones	$ 50,000	$ 58,000	$ 8,000	0.16
8	Mark Forest	$ 15,000	$ 21,000	$ 6,000	0.4
9	Mary Hill	$ 22,000	$ 29,000	$ 7,000	0.318182
10	Tom Brown	$ 40,000	$ 47,000	$ 7,000	0.175

The outcome in **Figure 3-14** is much easier to read.

Figure 3-14

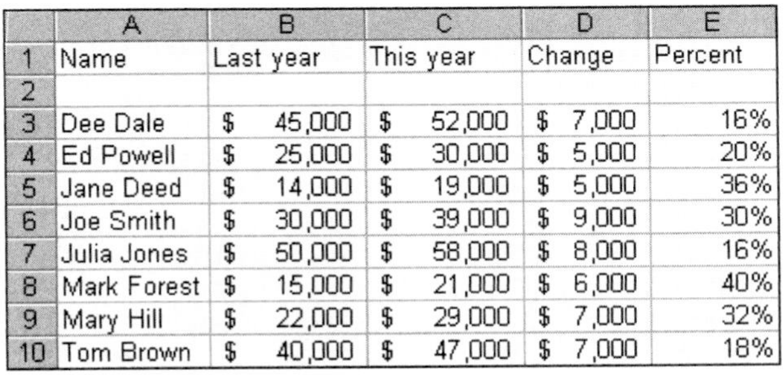

	A	B	C	D	E
1	Name	Last year	This year	Change	Percent
2					
3	Dee Dale	$ 45,000	$ 52,000	$ 7,000	16%
4	Ed Powell	$ 25,000	$ 30,000	$ 5,000	20%
5	Jane Deed	$ 14,000	$ 19,000	$ 5,000	36%
6	Joe Smith	$ 30,000	$ 39,000	$ 9,000	30%
7	Julia Jones	$ 50,000	$ 58,000	$ 8,000	16%
8	Mark Forest	$ 15,000	$ 21,000	$ 6,000	40%
9	Mary Hill	$ 22,000	$ 29,000	$ 7,000	32%
10	Tom Brown	$ 40,000	$ 47,000	$ 7,000	18%

Going from Horizontal to Vertical

By comparing rows, you have been doing calculations horizontally in the two-dimensional world of a spreadsheet. But you can also do vertical calculations. For the story on the mayor's cronies, you might want to know how much their salaries are costing taxpayers. For this, you want to total numbers in the columns.

You move the cursor to the box in **Figure 3-15** in which you want the total to appear. (By the way, the individual boxes in a spreadsheet are called "**cells.**")

You type the "=" again, then the word "SUM" and then the range of cells you want to total. In this case, the numbers start at B3 and end at

B10. So you type "=SUM(B3:B10)," as shown in **Figure 3-15,** putting a colon between the beginning location and the ending location.

Figure 3-15

	A	B	C	D	E
	SUM ▾ X ✓ =	=SUM(B3:B10)			
1	Name	Last year	This year	Change	Percent
2					
3	Dee Dale	$ 45,000	$ 52,000	$ 7,000	16%
4	Ed Powell	$ 25,000	$ 30,000	$ 5,000	20%
5	Jane Deed	$ 14,000	$ 19,000	$ 5,000	36%
6	Joe Smith	$ 30,000	$ 39,000	$ 9,000	30%
7	Julia Jones	$ 50,000	$ 58,000	$ 8,000	16%
8	Mark Forest	$ 15,000	$ 21,000	$ 6,000	40%
9	Mary Hill	$ 22,000	$ 29,000	$ 7,000	32%
10	Tom Brown	$ 40,000	$ 47,000	$ 7,000	18%
11					
12	Total	=SUM(B3:B10)			

When you hit "Enter," the total appears as in **Figure 3-16.**

Figure 3-16

	A	B	C	D	E
	B12 ▾ =	=SUM(B3:B10)			
1	Name	Last year	This year	Change	Percent
2					
3	Dee Dale	$ 45,000	$ 52,000	$ 7,000	16%
4	Ed Powell	$ 25,000	$ 30,000	$ 5,000	20%
5	Jane Deed	$ 14,000	$ 19,000	$ 5,000	36%
6	Joe Smith	$ 30,000	$ 39,000	$ 9,000	30%
7	Julia Jones	$ 50,000	$ 58,000	$ 8,000	16%
8	Mark Forest	$ 15,000	$ 21,000	$ 6,000	40%
9	Mary Hill	$ 22,000	$ 29,000	$ 7,000	32%
10	Tom Brown	$ 40,000	$ 47,000	$ 7,000	18%
11					
12	Total	$ 241,000			

Rather than repeating the formula for each column, do what you did when calculating differences in rows: Using the narrow cross, copy the formula horizontally, as shown in **Figure 3-17.**

Figure 3-17

B12	▼	=	=SUM(B3:B10)	
	A	B	C	D	E
1	Name	Last year	This year	Change	Percent
2					
3	Dee Dale	$ 45,000	$ 52,000	$ 7,000	16%
4	Ed Powell	$ 25,000	$ 30,000	$ 5,000	20%
5	Jane Deed	$ 14,000	$ 19,000	$ 5,000	36%
6	Joe Smith	$ 30,000	$ 39,000	$ 9,000	30%
7	Julia Jones	$ 50,000	$ 58,000	$ 8,000	16%
8	Mark Forest	$ 15,000	$ 21,000	$ 6,000	40%
9	Mary Hill	$ 22,000	$ 29,000	$ 7,000	32%
10	Tom Brown	$ 40,000	$ 47,000	$ 7,000	18%
11					
12	Total	$ 241,000			

Let go of the mouse button, and the result appears as shown in **Figure 3-18.**

Figure 3-18

D12	▼	=	=SUM(D3:D10)	
	A	B	C	D	E
1	Name	Last year	This year	Change	Percent
2					
3	Dee Dale	$ 45,000	$ 52,000	$ 7,000	16%
4	Ed Powell	$ 25,000	$ 30,000	$ 5,000	20%
5	Jane Deed	$ 14,000	$ 19,000	$ 5,000	36%
6	Joe Smith	$ 30,000	$ 39,000	$ 9,000	30%
7	Julia Jones	$ 50,000	$ 58,000	$ 8,000	16%
8	Mark Forest	$ 15,000	$ 21,000	$ 6,000	40%
9	Mary Hill	$ 22,000	$ 29,000	$ 7,000	32%
10	Tom Brown	$ 40,000	$ 47,000	$ 7,000	18%
11					
12	Total	$ 241,000	$ 295,000	$ 54,000	
13					

You might also want to determine how the average increase for the mayor's cronies compares to the average increase for all employees. There are two ways of looking at this. To compare the average percentage increase for the mayor's cronies, giving equal weight to each employee regardless of salary, you would average the percentages in column E and get 26 percent. (We will do an average later in this chapter.)

But if you wanted to calculate the percentage increase in the total amount of money paid to the cronies, you would calculate the difference in the rows. To do that, you would not average the percentages. You would calculate the percentage difference between the totals (C12 and B12) by subtracting B12 from C12, with the answer appearing in D12. Then you would divide D12 by B12. The result, shown in **Figure 3-19,** would be approximately 22 percent, or more than four times that of all employees.

Figure 3-19

E12 ▼	= =D12/B12			
	A	B	C	D	E
1	Name	Last year	This year	Change	Percent
2					
3	Dee Dale	$ 45,000	$ 52,000	$ 7,000	16%
4	Ed Powell	$ 25,000	$ 30,000	$ 5,000	20%
5	Jane Deed	$ 14,000	$ 19,000	$ 5,000	36%
6	Joe Smith	$ 30,000	$ 39,000	$ 9,000	30%
7	Julia Jones	$ 50,000	$ 58,000	$ 8,000	16%
8	Mark Forest	$ 15,000	$ 21,000	$ 6,000	40%
9	Mary Hill	$ 22,000	$ 29,000	$ 7,000	32%
10	Tom Brown	$ 40,000	$ 47,000	$ 7,000	18%
11					
12	Total	$ 241,000	$ 295,000	$ 54,000	22%

▼ Comparing Parts to the Sum

You might also want to see who got the biggest chunk of money out of the salary increases. If this were a city budget, you might want to see which department received the largest portion of the city budget. In either case, you want to compare the individual raises with the total amount of raises for each person. Thus, you want to compare D3 with D12, D4 with D12 and so on.

However, a spreadsheet is used to moving down a row at each calculation. Without some hint of what you want to do, the spreadsheet will compare D3 with D12 and then D4 with D13, which would be nonsense. The long and short of it is that we need to "anchor" D12.

Fortunately, spreadsheets give us an easy way to accomplish that. As shown in **Figure 3-20,** we anchor D12 by putting a dollar sign, "$," before the letter and a "$" sign before the number: "$D$12." The first dollar sign anchors the column, and the second dollar sign anchors the row. Now the spreadsheet knows to compare all the numbers in a column only with D12.

Figure 3-20

	A	B	C	D	E	F
	SUM	▼	✗ ✓ =	=D3/$D$12		
1	Name	Last year	This year	Change	Percent	Percent of Total
2						
3	Dee Dale	$ 45,000	$ 52,000	$ 7,000	16%	=D3/$D$12
4	Ed Powell	$ 25,000	$ 30,000	$ 5,000	20%	
5	Jane Deed	$ 14,000	$ 19,000	$ 5,000	36%	
6	Joe Smith	$ 30,000	$ 39,000	$ 9,000	30%	
7	Julia Jones	$ 50,000	$ 58,000	$ 8,000	16%	
8	Mark Forest	$ 15,000	$ 21,000	$ 6,000	40%	
9	Mary Hill	$ 22,000	$ 29,000	$ 7,000	32%	
10	Tom Brown	$ 40,000	$ 47,000	$ 7,000	18%	
11						
12	Total	$ 241,000	$ 295,000	$ 54,000	22%	

Press "Enter," and in **Figure 3-21** you obtain a new percentage of the total.

Figure 3-21

	A	B	C	D	E	F
1	Name	Last year	This year	Change	Percent	Percent of Total
2						
3	Dee Dale	$ 45,000	$ 52,000	$ 7,000	16%	0.12962963
4	Ed Powell	$ 25,000	$ 30,000	$ 5,000	20%	
5	Jane Deed	$ 14,000	$ 19,000	$ 5,000	36%	
6	Joe Smith	$ 30,000	$ 39,000	$ 9,000	30%	
7	Julia Jones	$ 50,000	$ 58,000	$ 8,000	16%	
8	Mark Forest	$ 15,000	$ 21,000	$ 6,000	40%	
9	Mary Hill	$ 22,000	$ 29,000	$ 7,000	32%	
10	Tom Brown	$ 40,000	$ 47,000	$ 7,000	18%	
11						
12	Total	$ 241,000	$ 295,000	$ 54,000	22%	

Again, copy the formula. Then use the percentage icon, and **Figure 3-22** shows the result.

Figure 3-22

	A	B	C	D	E	F
1	Name	Last year	This year	Change	Percent	Percent of Total
2						
3	Dee Dale	$ 45,000	$ 52,000	$ 7,000	16%	13%
4	Ed Powell	$ 25,000	$ 30,000	$ 5,000	20%	9%
5	Jane Deed	$ 14,000	$ 19,000	$ 5,000	36%	9%
6	Joe Smith	$ 30,000	$ 39,000	$ 9,000	30%	17%
7	Julia Jones	$ 50,000	$ 58,000	$ 8,000	16%	15%
8	Mark Forest	$ 15,000	$ 21,000	$ 6,000	40%	11%
9	Mary Hill	$ 22,000	$ 29,000	$ 7,000	32%	13%
10	Tom Brown	$ 40,000	$ 47,000	$ 7,000	18%	13%
11						
12	Total	$ 241,000	$ 295,000	$ 54,000	22%	

From this calculation you see that Joe Smith got the biggest chunk —
17 percent — of the raises.

Sorting the Results

Journalists generally want to put information in some kind of order. If
you were doing this with a large spreadsheet, you'd have to go through
hundreds of numbers to search for the highest percentage. Instead, a
spreadsheet allows you to **sort** the information rapidly. This brings us to
another bugaboo.

When you sort a spreadsheet, you want to keep all the information in
each row together. But a spreadsheet can make sorting so easy that a
journalist rushes past this important point.

You must outline the entire area to sort. All rows of numbers should
be highlighted. Many older versions of spreadsheets allowed you to sort
one column of information without moving the rest of the row. That
meant your percentages were suddenly scrambled and matched against
the wrong information. In newer versions, you can get into the same
problem by putting blank columns between columns of information
and ignoring the warnings that pop up.

Here you outline the entire area, as shown in **Figure 3-23,** leaving out
the labels of the columns. (We have placed a blank row between titles
and the labels so that it is easier to see the data. But if you wanted to
have the option of using the labels during the sorting, then you would
delete the blank row.)

Figure 3-23

	A	B	C	D	E	F
	A3 ▾		=	Dee Dale		
1	Name	Last year	This year	Change	Percent	Percent of Total
2						
3	Dee Dale	$ 45,000	$ 52,000	$ 7,000	16%	13%
4	Ed Powell	$ 25,000	$ 30,000	$ 5,000	20%	9%
5	Jane Deed	$ 14,000	$ 19,000	$ 5,000	36%	9%
6	Joe Smith	$ 30,000	$ 39,000	$ 9,000	30%	17%
7	Julia Jones	$ 50,000	$ 58,000	$ 8,000	16%	15%
8	Mark Forest	$ 15,000	$ 21,000	$ 6,000	40%	11%
9	Mary Hill	$ 22,000	$ 29,000	$ 7,000	32%	13%
10	Tom Brown	$ 40,000	$ 47,000	$ 7,000	18%	13%
11						
12	Total	$ 241,000	$ 295,000	$ 54,000	22%	

You then decide to go to the "Sort" command under "Data" in the menu shown in **Figure 3-24.**

Figure 3-24

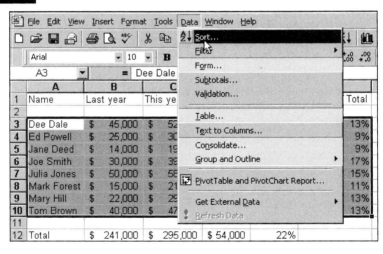

Clicking on "Sort" brings up the next screen, which gives the opportunity to choose which column to sort by and in what order. Lowest to highest is called "**ascending,**" and highest to lowest is called "**descending.**" As shown in **Figure 3-25,** you choose Column E and choose "descending."

Figure 3-25

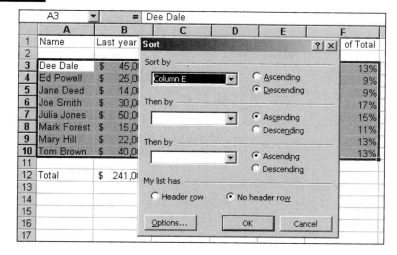

Now click on "OK." In **Figure 3-26** you see that Mark Forest received the highest percentage raise — 40 percent.

Figure 3-26

	A	B	C	D	E	F
1	Name	Last year	This year	Change	Percent	Percent of Total
2						
3	Mark Forest	$ 15,000	$ 21,000	$ 6,000	40%	11%
4	Jane Deed	$ 14,000	$ 19,000	$ 5,000	36%	9%
5	Mary Hill	$ 22,000	$ 29,000	$ 7,000	32%	13%
6	Joe Smith	$ 30,000	$ 39,000	$ 9,000	30%	17%
7	Ed Powell	$ 25,000	$ 30,000	$ 5,000	20%	9%
8	Tom Brown	$ 40,000	$ 47,000	$ 7,000	18%	13%
9	Julia Jones	$ 50,000	$ 58,000	$ 8,000	16%	15%
10	Dee Dale	$ 45,000	$ 52,000	$ 7,000	16%	13%
11						
12	Total	$ 241,000	$ 295,000	$ 54,000	22%	
13						
14						
15						

At this point, your initial work is done, and it's time to start planning your interviews with the mayor, the cronies and regular employees of the city. At the same time, you should start planning your graphics and photos to go with the story.

▼ Using Average and Median for Better Accuracy

To deal with numbers, you should know three of the most common ways of summarizing a collection of numbers: mean, median and **mode.** *Mean* is what is commonly called the **average. Median** is defined as the middle value, or the point at which half the numbers fall above and half the numbers fall below. (If there is a tie, it gets a little tricky, but a spreadsheet can work out the calculation for you.) *Mode* is the most frequent value in the database or the value most frequently seen when you look at the data.

Neill Borowski, who has practiced and taught computer-assisted reporting at The Philadelphia Inquirer, used a good example of this at a national conference. He said baseball players' salaries outraged fans because fans always heard the average salary was $1.2 million. But the median salary was $500,000, and the mode, or the most frequent salary, was $109,000.

Those numbers indicate that there are a few players making really, really big money. The middle value, the salary amount that half the salaries exceed and half the salaries fall below, was $500,000. If you asked all baseball players for a count of hands for each salary, the largest number (the mode, not the majority) of hands would go up for $109,000. (Okay, it's still a lot of money, but not as much as you thought, and it's being made by people who generally make most of their money in 10 years or less.)

Journalists want to make sure they represent numbers as fairly and accurately as possible, and these three ways of looking at numbers give them a chance to do so. If a journalist obtains a set of salaries or house prices or test scores, he or she needs to consider what the fairest representation is. If the numbers are relatively close together, the **mean** (or average) is a reasonable way to summarize them. But if the numbers are spread out, a journalist doesn't want a few bad apples, or very rich apples, to distort the summary.

Let's stay on the subject of sports and take a look at a basketball team with a former superstar such as Michael Jordan. (You could select any names for this example.) **Figure 3-27** shows a fictional account of what they make in each quarter of a game.

Figure 3-27

	A	B	C
1	Player	Salary	
2			
3	Jordan	60000	
4	Pippen	70000	
5	Rodman	40000	
6	Longley	30000	
7	Harper	50000	
8			
9	✛		
10			

First, we will get the average of what they make. You get an average by going to B8 and typing the formula "=AVERAGE(B3:B7)," as shown in **Figure 3-28,** and hitting "Enter."

Figure 3-28

	A	B	C
1	Player	Salary	
2			
3	Jordan	60000	
4	Pippen	70000	
5	Rodman	40000	
6	Longley	30000	
7	Harper	50000	
8	Average	=AVERAGE(B3:B7)	
9		✛	

Next, we will get the median of what they make. You obtain a median by going to B9 and typing the formula "=MEDIAN(B3:B7)" as shown in **Figure 3-29.**

Figure 3-29

	A	B	C
1	Player	Salary	
2			
3	Jordan	60000	
4	Pippen	70000	
5	Rodman	40000	
6	Longley	30000	
7	Harper	50000	
8	Average	50000	
9	Median	=MEDIAN(B3:B7)	
10			

At this point, there is no difference between average and median because there are two salaries higher than $50,000 and two salaries lower than $50,000. Now we look back at our figures and we realize we left a zero off the superstar's salary. We replace Jordan's $60,000 with $600,000, as in **Figure 3-30.**

Figure 3-30

	A	B	
1	Player	Salary	
2			
3	Jordan	600000	
4	Pippen	70000	
5	Rodman	40000	
6	Longley	30000	
7	Harper	50000	
8	Average	158000	
9	Median	50000	
10			

Notice how the formula immediately changes the result in the average row. The median does not change because there are still two salaries higher and two salaries lower than $50,000. This is an extreme example, but you can see that the median more fairly represents what the players make.

▼ Interpreting Outliers

In this example, Jordan would be considered an **"outlier."** In social
research parlance, an *outlier* is a number that is out on the edge of the
chart, way up on the top of the chart, or way down at the bottom of the
chart.

These measurements — average and median — help you quickly identify an outlier. You could say that Jordan, the chief executive of the corporation, makes 12 times as much as the median wage.

But, quite often, if you examine a few databases closely, you begin to
regard outliers with healthy suspicion. Often outliers are too good to be
true. They frequently turn out to be the product of data entry errors
(which will be examined in a later chapter). The usual disappointment
is that someone put in an extra zero, for example, and Jordan's game
quarter salary actually is $60,000.

Also, social researchers suggest that you look carefully at the outliers
and possibly discard them, especially if you expect to work with averages. That doesn't mean you can't bring the outliers back for a repeat
performance later. You might be looking at census data and notice that
one county has highly unusual numbers. So you examine all the counties but that one in your first analysis and then look at all the counties
together to see how that one county can distort the numbers.

Averages can also hide important information. At the San Jose
Mercury, in a classic story, reporters obtained an electronic file from
the city that included the times of the alarms and the times of fire
trucks' arrival at the scene of fires. The fire department claimed that its
average response time was 4.5 minutes, half a minute under the maximum time it allowed itself to get to any fire.

Reporters Betty Barnacle and Chris Schmitt found the fire department
wasn't wrong about its average. What the fire department didn't say —
but the numbers showed — was that on one-fourth of its calls, the fire
department violated its five-minute guideline. With his analysis, Schmitt
ensured that the story not only related an isolated occurrence, but also
showed a pattern of problems.

▼ **CAR Wars**

When a court reporter at The Hartford Courant, Jack Ewing, and I looked at racial disparities in bail for criminal defendants in Connecticut, we examined the average bail for blacks and Hispanics versus whites. However, on the advice of some good social science researchers, we limited the bail to amounts above zero and equal to or below $100,000. (We got rid of zero because that meant the person did not have any bail set. We held to $100,000 or below because there were a few amounts above $100,000 that could distort the results.) We found that black and Hispanic males, on average, received much higher bail — nearly double — than whites for the same kind of felony. Then, we went back and looked at the outliers. It turned out that an unusual number of high bail amounts were being given to blacks in one courthouse. In fact, blacks were getting higher bail amounts — as much as $1,000,000 — for drug charges than some whites were getting for drug charges or murder.

Later, a judge in New Haven acknowledged that he was giving out high bail to those accused of drug offenses because he didn't think the accused spent enough time in jail once they were convicted. Thus, his solution was to lock up the presumed innocent. Unfortunately, the judge was contributing to his own frustration because when he kept people in jail awaiting trial, it created prison overcrowding — which led to the early release of those found guilty and serving time. He was unaware, however, that he also was creating racial disparities.

Once again, we learned how numbers and math can not only provide context, but also can tip us to good stories. Using a spreadsheet to do a few calculations, it's possible to find patterns, make better comparisons and discover the unusual.

Brant Houston, executive director of IRE and NICAR

Chapter Checklist

- Spreadsheets can help you do calculations faster and more easily.

- Spreadsheets use letters to identify columns and numbers to identify rows.

- For calculations, spreadsheets allow you to use column letters and row numbers to create formulas.

- Percentage difference often provides a more fair comparison.

- When you are comparing the parts of a calculation with the sum, don't forget to "anchor" the sum.

- When you sort, make sure to highlight the entire range of numbers that you want to sort.

 Your Turn to Practice

1 Get a list of names and salaries from your city, county or state in electronic form or in hard copy.

2 Get a part of a city, county or state budget in electronic form or in hard copy. Make sure you get two years' worth.

3 Put one or both datasets into a worksheet in Excel.

4 Sort in descending order, using the salary. Sort in descending order, using the amount of each budget.

5 Calculate the difference in the budget years. Calculate the percentage difference.

6 Calculate the total, average and median for the salaries.

7 Find out which department has the largest percentage of the budget.

> **www**
>
> For more exercises in downloading and importing, go to
> **www.ire.org/carbook/chapter3**

CHAPTER 4

Spreadsheets, Part 2

More Math That Matters

"We decided to obtain a list of the delinquent taxpayers, analyze it and publish it in a format that people could under-stand. . . . The top 10 real estate debtors combined owed more than $6.4 million, but the city is unlikely to collect any of that soon."

— **The Waterbury Republican American in Connecticut**

"Simply summing the two columns showed what the campaign spent and took in. . . . Overall we found at least $10,000 in unaccounted funds and several violations of state election law."

— **The Courier-Post in New Jersey**

"Simply put, a ratio study compares assessed values with actual prices properties sell for. . . . We got a county overseer to admit that his assessors were murmuring privately about 'so many mistakes . . . it's unbelievable.'"

— **The Tribune Review in Pittsburgh, Pennsylvania**

In recent years, journalists have gone far beyond basic math. They calculate a rate and a ratio, they filter and reconfigure their data to make it more meaningful, and they visualize using charts and graphs. Most often, they do this in spreadsheet software, but more journalists are using statistical software such as SPSS and SAS and applying social research methods espoused by Philip Meyer, a pioneer in database analysis and author of "Precision Journalism." (See this book's appendix on the use of statistical software.)

In the previous chapter, we looked at the basic math a journalist needs to know and how spreadsheets make doing that math faster and easier. This chapter expands on the basic math and statistics skills for doing better journalism.

▼ Rates

Sarah Cohen, a Pulitzer Prize–winning reporter and former government statistics expert, says, "Rates are used to level the playing field." **Rates** allow you to make comparisons that are more fair and accurate — just as the calculations of median or percentage differences do. Just comparing raw numbers can wrongly and unfairly distort the differences on such topics as illnesses, traffic accidents and crimes. Ten traffic accidents in an intersection through which only 100 cars pass a day have a far different impact than 10 traffic accidents at an intersection through which 10,000 cars pass a day.

Consequently, journalists now calculate rates on many topics such as transportation accidents, taxes, deaths, loans, arrests and disease. Let's take a look at crime data as an example.

If you were to look at crime statistics on murder in cities with populations greater than 250,000, it would probably not surprise you that Chicago leads with 666 murders and New York is close behind with 649 (see **Figure 4-1**). After all, Chicago is a city with more than 2.8 million people, and New York has the largest population with 8 million people.

Figure 4-1

	A	B	C
	C2 ▼ = 666		
	A	**B**	**C**
1	**City**	**Population**	**Murders**
2	Chicago	2,896,016	666
3	New York	8,023,018	649
4	Los Angeles	3,763,486	588
5	Detroit	956,283	395
6	Philadelphia	1,518,302	309
7	Houston	1,997,965	267
8	Baltimore	660,826	256
9	Dallas	1,215,553	240
10	Washington D.C.	571,822	232

But would that really tell you how dangerous Chicago is as compared to other cities? Would it give you an idea of the chances of being murdered in Chicago compared to another city? Not really. One way to get a better idea is to use a per capita figure or a rate. Now that you know formulas, you know how easy it is to put a calculation in a spreadsheet.

In **Figure 4-2,** you divide the number of murders in each city (C2 for Chicago) by each city's population (B2). This would give you a per capita (per person) figure, but all those decimals would prevent it from being meaningful to a reader or viewer.

Figure 4-2

	A	B	C	D
	D2 ▾ = =C2/B2			
1	City	Populatio Murders		Per Capita
2	Chicago	2,896,016	666	0.00023
3	New York	8,023,018	649	
4	Los Angeles	3,763,486	588	
5	Detroit	956,283	395	
6	Philadelphia	1,518,302	309	

To make it more understandable, you need to move the decimal point to the right by multiplying the per capita figure by 100,000 to get the rate per 100,000 persons. The multiplier is often a question of judgment on what makes sense, such as the population size and the number of occurrences in relation to the population (see **Figure 4-3**).

Figure 4-3

	A	B	C	D
	SUM ▾ ✗ ✓ = =C2/B2*100000			
1	City	Population	Murders	Per 100,000
2	Chicago	2,896,016	666	=C2/B2*100000
3	New York	8,023,018	649	
4	Los Angeles	3,763,486	588	
5	Detroit	956,283	395	
6	Philadelphia	1,518,302	309	

Then, by multiplying by 100,000, you get 22.99711, as shown in **Figure 4-4.**

Figure 4-4

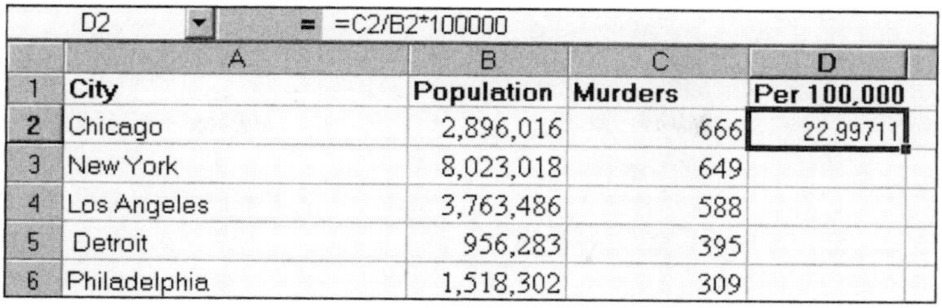

	A	B	C	D
	D2 ▼ = =C2/B2*100000			
1	City	Population	Murders	Per 100,000
2	Chicago	2,896,016	666	22.99711
3	New York	8,023,018	649	
4	Los Angeles	3,763,486	588	
5	Detroit	956,283	395	
6	Philadelphia	1,518,302	309	

After you get the formula, copy it down the column to obtain figures for each city. See **Figure 4-5.** (A helpful hint: Also click on the "," in the Tool Bar to reduce the decimals to only two places. This should automatically appear in your Tool Bar, as in **Figure 4-5.**)

Figure 4-5

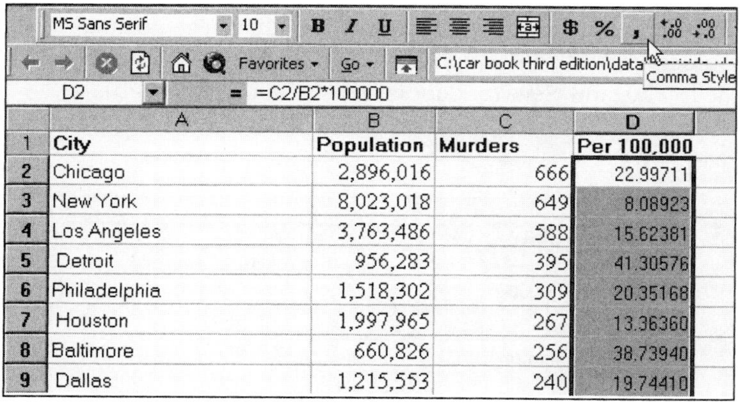

MS Sans Serif 10 **B** *I* U $ % , Comma Style

D2 ▼ = =C2/B2*100000

	A	B	C	D
1	City	Population	Murders	Per 100,000
2	Chicago	2,896,016	666	22.99711
3	New York	8,023,018	649	8.08923
4	Los Angeles	3,763,486	588	15.62381
5	Detroit	956,283	395	41.30576
6	Philadelphia	1,518,302	309	20.35168
7	Houston	1,997,965	267	13.36360
8	Baltimore	660,826	256	38.73940
9	Dallas	1,215,553	240	19.74410

Now sort the information in descending order by Column D as shown in **Figure 4-6.** (Don't forget to select the entire data range so that columns are not accidentally sorted out of order.)

Figure 4-6

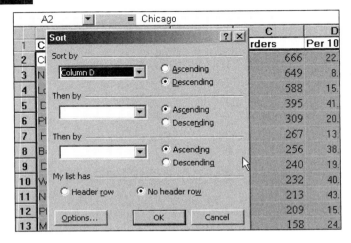

You will find, as shown in **Figure 4-7,** that New Orleans has the most murders per 100,000 people at 43.98. Chicago falls near the bottom of the top 10, and New York does not even make the top 10.

Figure 4-7

	A	B	C	D
	D2 ▼ = =C2/B2*100000			
	A	B	C	D
1	City	Population	Murders	Per 100,000
2	New Orleans	484,289	213	43.98
3	Detroit	956,283	395	41.31
4	Washington D.C.	571,822	232	40.57
5	Baltimore	660,826	256	38.74
6	Atlanta	426,511	144	33.76
7	Newark	275,823	90	32.63
8	Memphis	655,898	158	24.09
9	Chicago	2,896,016	666	23.00
10	Buffalo	293,187	64	21.83

▼ Ranking

Once you have the worksheet organized this way, you might want to rank the cities — that is, list the cities from high to low based on your work. To do this, you first create a new column by highlighting column

A and then clicking on "Insert" and moving the cursor to "Columns," as in **Figure 4-8.**

Figure 4-8

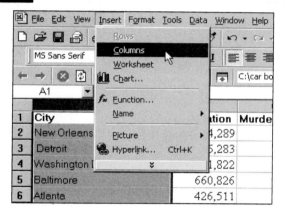

By clicking on "Columns," you get a new column to the left of the cities as in **Figure 4-9,** and you can type in a column title, "Rank."

Figure 4-9

	A	B	C	D	E
	A1	= Rank			
1	Rank	City	Population	Murders	Per 100,000
2		New Orleans	484,289	213	43.98
3		Detroit	956,283	395	41.31
4		Washington D.C.	571,822	232	40.57
5		Baltimore	660,826	256	38.74
6		Atlanta	426,511	144	33.76
7		Newark	275,823	90	32.63

Now type "1" in A2 and "2" in A3 as shown in **Figure 4-10.**

Figure 4-10

	A	B	C	D	E
	A3	▼	= 2		
1	Rank	City	Population	Murders	Per 100,000
2	1	New Orleans	484,289	213	43.98
3	2	Detroit	956,283	395	41.31
4		Washington D.C.	571,822	232	40.57
5		Baltimore	660,826	256	38.74
6		Atlanta	426,511	144	33.76
7		Newark	275,823	90	32.63

Highlight both A2 and A3, and place the cursor in the lower right-hand corner of A3 as shown in **Figure 4-11** so you can see the narrow cross.

Figure 4-11

	A	B	C	D
1	Rank	City	Population	Murders
2	1	New Orleans	484,289	213
3	2	Detroit	956,283	395
4		Washington D.C.	571,822	232
5		Baltimore	660,826	256

Double-click on the narrow cross, and you will have a ranking for each city, as shown in **Figure 4-12.** This allows you to give readers or viewers an idea of how their city compares to other cities.

Figure 4-12

	A	B	C	D	E
1	Rank	City	Population	Murders	Per 100,000
2	1	New Orleans	484,289	213	43.98
3	2	Detroit	956,283	395	41.31
4	3	Washington D.C.	571,822	232	40.57
5	4	Baltimore	660,826	256	38.74
6	5	Atlanta	426,511	144	33.76
7	6	Newark	275,823	90	32.63
8	7	Memphis	655,898	158	24.09
9	8	Chicago	2,896,016	666	23.00

▼Filtering

After creating rates and ranks for all the cities, you might want to compare only the largest cities. Without creating a new worksheet, you can use the "Filter" function of the spreadsheet. That is, you can **filter** in or filter out the data you want depending on the criteria.

To filter, first highlight the column through which you want to filter — that is, the prime criterion for your filter. In this case, it is Column C: Population, as shown in **Figure 4-13.**

Figure 4-13

	C1	▼	= Population	
	A	B	C	D
1	Rank	City	Population	Murders
2	1	New Orleans	484,289	
3	2	Detr	956,283	
4	3	Washington D.C.	571,822	
5	4	Baltimore	660,826	

Then go to the Menu Bar to "Data," as you did for "Sort." Except this time, choose "Filter" and then "AutoFilter," as shown in **Figure 4-14.**

Figure 4-14

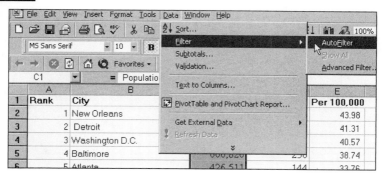

When you click on "AutoFilter," you will notice that a small arrow appears next to the word "Population" in C1, as in **Figure 4-15.**

Figure 4-15

	A	B	C	D
	C1	▼	= Population	
	A	B	Populatio ▼	Murders
1	Rank	City		
2	1	New Orleans	484,289	
3	2	Detroit	956,283	
4	3	Washington D.C.	571,822	
5	4	Baltimore	660,826	

Click on that arrow and then place the cursor on "Custom," which will let you choose how you will "filter" the worksheet, as in **Figure 4-16.**

Figure 4-16

	A	B	C	D
	C1	▼	= Population	
	A	B	Populatio ▼	Murders
1	Rank	City	(All)	
2	1	New Orleans	(Top 10...)	213
3	2	Detroit	(Custom...)	395
4	3	Washington D.C.	251,648 / 254,664	232
5	4	Baltimore	255,551	256
6	5	Atlanta	257,739 / 259,908	144

Click on the arrow next to "equals" in the box that pops up and choose "is greater than or equal to," as in **Figure 4-17.**

Figure 4-17

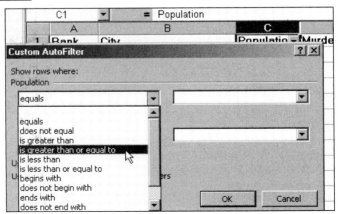

Now click on that and go to the box directly across from "is greater than or equal to" and type "1,000,000," as in **Figure 4-18.** (Note that this box uses Boolean logic — and, or, not, as we saw in Chapter 2 — which allows you to employ more specific criteria.) Note that this kind of filtering of information based on a criterion will be discussed again in the chapters on database managers. In database software, filtering is known as choosing the criteria or using a "where" statement.

Figure 4-18

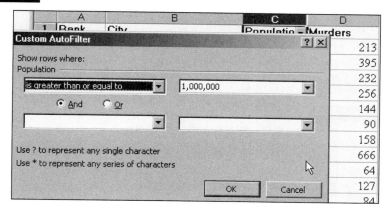

Click on "OK," and you have a much smaller set of data comparing cities with populations of 1,000,000 people or more. Note that Chicago is now back on top and New York is near the bottom, as shown in **Figure 4-19.**

Figure 4-19

	C1	▼	= Population		
	A	B	C	D	E
1	Rank	City	Populatio ▼	Murders	Per 100,000
9	8	Chicago	2,896,016	666	23.00
13	12	Philadelphia	1,518,302	309	20.35
14	13	Dallas	1,215,553	240	19.74
19	18	Los Angeles	3,763,486	588	15.62
20	19	Phoenix	1,366,542	209	15.29
21	20	Houston	1,997,965	267	13.36
23	22	Las Vegas Metropolitan Polic	1,117,763	133	11.90
37	36	San Antonio	1,170,622	100	8.54
40	39	New York	8,023,018	649	8.09
52	51	San Diego	1,246,136	50	4.01

▼ Ratios

A **ratio** is another powerful calculation for making comparisons, and it can be easier to understand. For example, a ratio can provide one number that can show the difference in the chances of being in an accident, getting a disease or receiving a grant.

Journalists looking into home mortgage loans have used ratio to illuminate the disparity in bank loans made to whites and to minorities. If 30 percent of black applicants are denied loans and 10 percent of whites are denied loans, a ratio comes in handy.

Let's calculate only this ratio in a spreadsheet, as shown in **Figure 4-20.** Type "Black" in A1, "White" in B1, and "Ratio" in C1. Type "30" in A2 and "10" in B2. In C2, type "=A2/B2" and hit "Enter." You now have your ratio of 3 to 1.

Figure 4-20

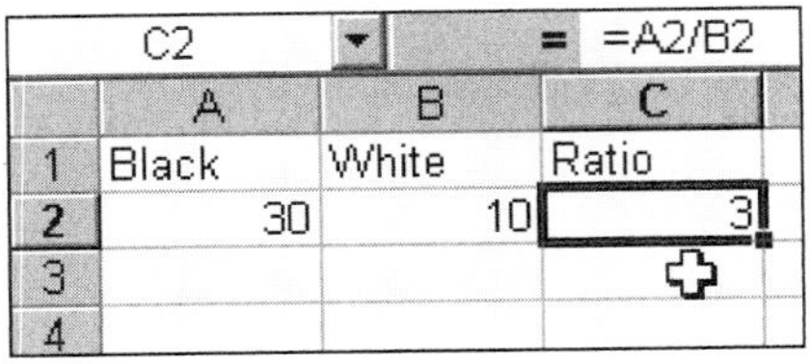

Now you can convey the disparity more simply by saying that three times as many blacks as whites are denied loans.

Rich Gordon, a journalism professor at Northwestern University, shared a classic example of the use of ratios when he worked at The Miami Herald in the 1990s.

The sheriff in Broward County in Florida said he wanted to go after illegal drug dealers as opposed to arresting those who only possessed the drugs. Gordon obtained data on drug arrests of dealers and users in counties in Florida so that he could see if the sheriff was indeed focusing on dealers and also how the sheriff compared to other county sheriffs. This is the actual data used by Gordon, so the populations and even the name of a county are different. Column C shows the total arrests for sales and Column D the total arrests for possession (see **Figure 4-21**).

Figure 4-21

E4	▼	=	
	A	B	C	D
1	COUNTY	POP	TOTALSALE	TOT_POSS
2	FLORIDA	13,195,952	20,566	42,506
3	ALACHUA	183,773	105	520
4	BAKER	18,905	29	37
5	BAY	128,575	261	386
6	BRADFORD	22,749	18	86
7	BREVARD	409,370	396	1,372
8	BROWARD	1,278,384	2,700	6,687
9	CALHOUN	11,216	21	0

You can find the user/dealer arrest ratio by dividing the number of those arrested for possession by those arrested for dealing drugs, D2/C2, as shown in **Figure 4-22,** and hitting "Enter."

Figure 4-22

E2	▼	=	=D2/C2	
	A	B	C	D	E
1	COUNTY	POP	TOTALSALE	TOT_POSS	RATIO
2	FLORIDA	13,195,952	20,566	42,506	2.066809
3	ALACHUA	183,773	105	520	
4	BAKER	18,905	29	37	
5	BAY	128,575	261	386	
6	BRADFORD	22,749	18	86	

To get rid of all but two decimal places, click on the "," in the Tool Bar. Of course, in some cases you might not want to use any decimal places. By sorting the data in descending order — based on ratios — Gordon also found that the sheriff had not distinguished himself in any major way from sheriffs in other counties (see **Figure 4-23**).

Figure 4-23

	E13	▼	= =D13/C13	
	A	B	C	D	E
1	COUNTY	POP	TOTALSALE	TOT_POSS	RATIO
2	ALACHUA	183,773	105	520	4.95
3	LEON	198,269	153	734	4.80
4	BRADFORD	22,749	18	86	4.78
5	ST. JOHNS	86,118	50	213	4.26
6	MARTIN	103,083	95	381	4.01
7	NASSAU	44,957	13	51	3.92
8	BREVARD	409,370	396	1,372	3.46
9	VOLUSIA	376,695	509	1,754	3.45
10	PALM BEACH	883,044	808	2,557	3.16
11	SARASOTA	279,577	284	889	3.13
12	PINELLAS	855,763	1,061	2,998	2.83
13	BROWARD	1,278,384	2,700	6,687	2.48
14	POLK	414,700	511	1,179	2.31
15	DADE	1,961,694	3,907	9,014	2.31
16	GLADES	7,922	11	24	2.18

For a further look at the sheriff's performance, you can also obtain a rate of possession arrests per 10,000 people. Using 10,000 works as a multiplier because of the population range of the counties. Divide the number of possession arrests by population and multiply by 10,000. If you copy the formula and then sort based on Column F, you will see in **Figure 4-24** that the Broward County sheriff's arrest rate of those who possess drugs is among the highest in the state.

Figure 4-24

	A	B	C	D	E	F
1	COUNTY	POP	TOTALSALE	TOT_POSS	RATIO	RATE
2	CHARLOTTE	11,557	85	123	1.45	106.43
3	MONROE	79,536	389	427	1.10	53.69
4	BROWARD	1,278,384	2,700	6,687	2.48	52.31
5	VOLUSIA	376,695	509	1,754	3.45	46.56
6	DADE	1,961,694	3,907	9,014	2.31	45.95
7	COLUMBIA	43,534	114	186	1.63	42.73
8	BRADFORD	22,749	18	86	4.78	37.80

▼ Subtotals

Another powerful way of summarizing information is to do subtotals of different categories. Often data comes in individual records that can be grouped into categories and subtotaled. Journalists do this for many topics, frequently for campaign finance reports. In this next example, we look at a sample of large contributions made by the Exxon Corporation (now ExxonMobil) to the Democratic and Republican parties over the past decade (see **Figure 4-25**).

Figure 4-25

	A	B	C	D
A1	▼	= EXXON CORPORATION		
1	EXXON CORPORATION	$15,000.00	RNC REPUBLICAN NATIONAL STATE ELECTIONS C	REP
2	EXXON CORPORATION	$15,000.00	DCCC BUILDING FUND ACCOUNT #1	DEM
3	EXXON CORPORATION	$15,000.00	DCCC NON FEDERAL ACCOUNT #1	DEM
4	EXXON CORPORATION	$20,000.00	NRSC - NONFEDERAL	REP
5	EXXON CORPORATION	$25,000.00	NRSC - BUILDING FUND	REP
6	EXXON CORPORATION	$25,000.00	NRSC - BUILDING FUND	REP
7	EXXON CORPORATION	$10,000.00	NRCCC - NONFEDERAL ACCOUNT	REP
8	EXXON CORPORATION	$10,000.00	NRCCC - NONFEDERAL ACCOUNT	REP

By inserting a row above row 1, we can type in column titles that label each column. Then using "Subtotals" under "Data" in the Menu Bar, we can see how much Exxon gave to the different committees of the parties (see **Figure 4-26**).

Figure 4-26

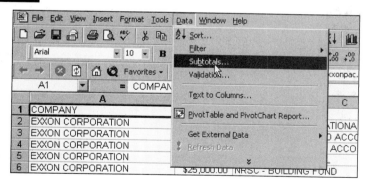

After clicking on "Subtotals," we get a choice on how to obtain the subtotal for each committee. In the first window, under "At each change in," we choose "Committee" as in **Figure 4-27.**

Figure 4-27

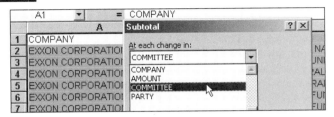

Under "Use function" we select "Sum." See **Figure 4-28.** This means we want to sum (or total) the amount that each committee received.

Figure 4-28

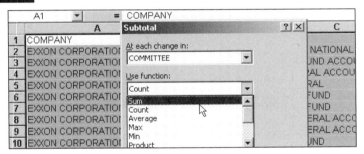

Under "Add subtotal to" we choose "Amount" as in **Figure 4-29.** This means that we want to add up the amount for each committee.

Figure 4-29

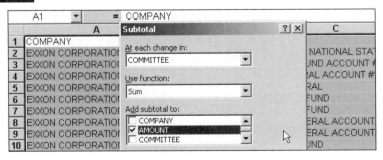

Then we click on "OK," and there is a subtotal for each committee, as shown in **Figure 4-30.**

Figure 4-30

1 2 3		A	B	C
	1	COMPANY	AMOUNT	COMMITTEE
	2	EXXON CORPORATION	$15,000.00	RNC REPUBLICAN NATIONAL STATE ELECTIONS C
	3		$15,000.00	**RNC REPUBLICAN NATIONAL STATE ELECTIONS**
	4	EXXON CORPORATION	$15,000.00	DCCC BUILDING FUND ACCOUNT #1
	5		$15,000.00	**DCCC BUILDING FUND ACCOUNT #1 Total**
	6	EXXON CORPORATION	$15,000.00	DCCC NON FEDERAL ACCOUNT #1
	7		$15,000.00	**DCCC NON FEDERAL ACCOUNT #1 Total**
	8	EXXON CORPORATION	$20,000.00	NRSC - NONFEDERAL
	9		$20,000.00	**NRSC - NONFEDERAL Total**
	10	EXXON CORPORATION	$25,000.00	NRSC - BUILDING FUND
	11	EXXON CORPORATION	$25,000.00	NRSC - BUILDING FUND
	12		$50,000.00	**NRSC - BUILDING FUND Total**

If we want to simplify this and see just the subtotals, we go to the left-hand side of the screen and click on the small "2" in **Figure 4-31.** This collapses the figure into just the subtotals.

Figure 4-31

1 2 3		A	B	C
	1	COMPANY	AMOUNT	COMMITTEE
	3		$15,000.00	**RNC REPUBLICAN NATIONAL STATE ELECTIO**
	5		$15,000.00	**DCCC BUILDING FUND ACCOUNT #1 Total**
	7		$15,000.00	**DCCC NON FEDERAL ACCOUNT #1 Total**
	9		$20,000.00	**NRSC - NONFEDERAL Total**
	12		$50,000.00	**NRSC - BUILDING FUND Total**
	15		$20,000.00	**NRCCC - NONFEDERAL ACCOUNT Total**

We could repeat this procedure if we wanted to know how much Exxon gave to each party. But in this case we need to sort the data by party first, as in **Figure 4-32,** for this to work. Remember that to do a sort on a column, it must be subtotaled first.

Figure 4-32

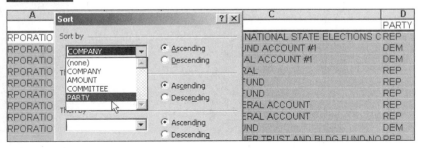

After sorting by "Party," we choose "Party," "Sum" and "Amount" in our "Subtotals" screen, as in **Figure 4-33.**

Figure 4-33

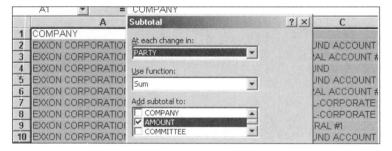

Then we hit "OK," and then "2," and we see how much more Exxon gave to the Republican Party and Democratic Party as in **Figure 4-34.**

Figure 4-34

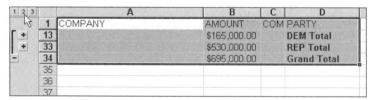

▼ Pivot Tables

Using a **Pivot Table** is like using "Subtotals," but it can take you much further in your analysis. It not only gives you subtotals, but the percentage of the total that each subtotal represents. You might see this in survey data published in a newspaper, but let's examine the Exxon contributions again and find not only the amount that Exxon gave to each party, but also the percentages of the total.

First, go to "Data" on the Menu Bar and click on "Pivot Tables," as shown in **Figure 4-35.**

Figure 4-35

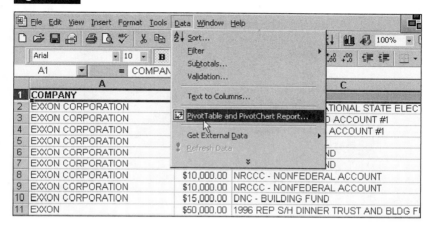

Click on "Next," since the data is in Excel, and you want to create a Pivot Table. Excel will automatically choose the range of *all* your data, and you will want to double-check that the range is accurate. In this example (see **Figure 4-36**), it should be A1 though D31.

Figure 4-36

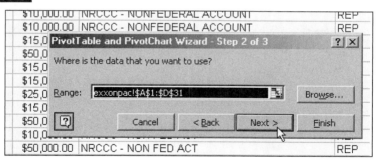

The next screen will give you the option of creating a new worksheet, which you should do, and it also allows you to choose the way to analyze the data by clicking on "Layout," as shown in **Figure 4-37.**

Figure 4-37

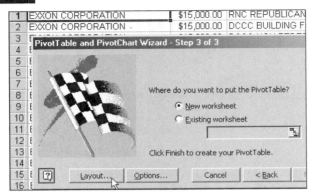

After clicking on "Layout," you get a screen on which you choose what rows and columns you plan to have in your new worksheet. Before making your selections, visualize how you want your answer to appear. You want to put the category Party (for which you will do totals) in the Row, and you will do the totals in the Data area (see **Figure 4-38**).

Figure 4-38

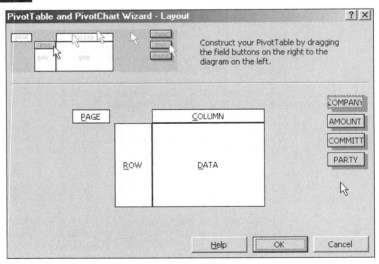

Click and drag "Party" to the Row section of the layout figure, because we want to know the total given by Exxon to each party. Then click and drag "Amount" to the Data area, where it will automatically say "Sum of Amount" (see **Figure 4-39**).

Figure 4-39

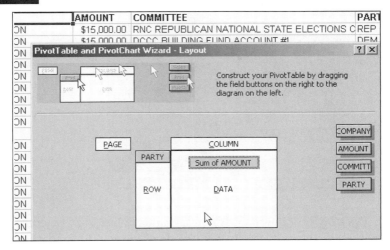

So far, this probably makes sense after doing Subtotals. But to get the percentage of the total that Exxon gave to each party, you must go through some extra steps. Now drag "Amount" to the Data area again, and you get a second box called "Sum of Amount2" (see **Figure 4-40**).

Figure 4-40

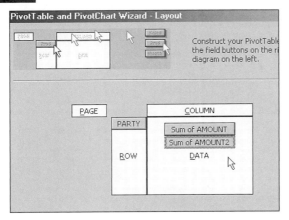

Double-click on "Sum of Amount2," and a new screen will appear. As you can see in **Figure 4-41,** you can change the function on the Sum of Amount2, but, more important, you have other "Options." Click there.

Figure 4-41

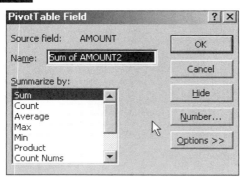

Click under "Show data as normal" and choose "% of column" because you want to get the percentage of the grand total of the amount given (see **Figure 4-42**).

Figure 4-42

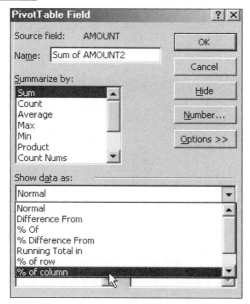

Click on "OK" to return to the Layout screen, and click on "OK" there to return to the original Pivot Table screen (see **Figure 4-43**).

Figure 4-43

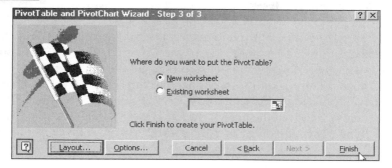

Now click on "Finish" and you have your answer. Exxon gave more than 75 percent of its large contributions to the Republican party, as shown in **Figure 4-44.**

Figure 4-44

	A	B	C	D
1		Drop Page Fields Here		
2				
3	PARTY ▾	Data ▾	Total	
4	DEM	Sum of AMOUNT	165000	
5		Sum of AMOUNT2	23.74%	
6	REP	Sum of AMOUNT	530000	
7		Sum of AMOUNT2	76.26%	✚
8	Total Sum of AMOUNT		695000	
9	Total Sum of AMOUNT2		100.00%	

You can do many other kinds of analyses with a Pivot Table, but this gives you an idea of its potential.

Both subtotals and Pivot Tables are good preparation for working with database manager software. With each tool, you are "grouping together" similar kinds of information and totaling the amount. In a database manager, which handles many more records, this is known as the "Group By" function, and in a database manager you would "Group By" party in the previous example and "Sum" the amounts.

▼ Charts and Graphs

There is one last activity to do that can make all the difference in spreadsheets: displaying the results of your analysis graphically. By using graphics effectively, you can see differences instantly and you don't have to slog through columns and columns of calculations.

Spreadsheets permit you to quickly place information into bar charts, pie charts and other kinds of charts. In this example, the different percentage increases in salaries of cronies might go into a bar chart.

If you want to do this, spreadsheets will make your work much easier. In this case, you could chart the dataset of cronies to see which employee received the highest percentages. First, highlight the "Name" column. Then, holding down the control key, move the cursor to the "Percent" (of raises) column and highlight that column.

Then click on what is called a "Chart Wizard" icon. A Chart Wizard helps you select the kind of chart you want to create. The arrow in **Figure 4-45** points out the icon.

Figure 4-45

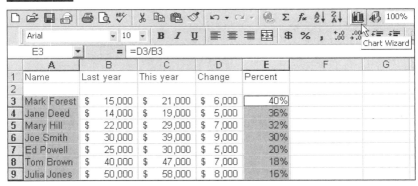

Click on the icon. The wizard then leads you through a series of steps in which you choose the kind of chart you want to create. In **Figure 4-46,** the wizard has highlighted the "Column" chart for you.

Figure 4-46

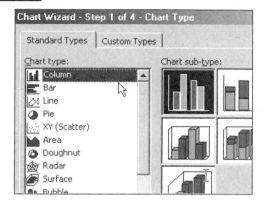

Continue along the steps the wizard lays out for you, and you will see a chart that graphically displays your information, as in **Figure 4-47.** Furthermore, it is a chart that you can enlarge, move around or copy and paste. (Note that you can save the chart in its own worksheet.)

Figure 4-47

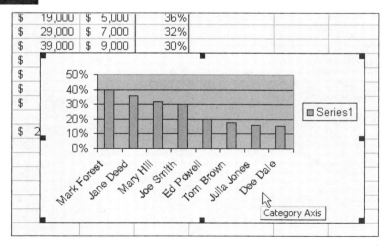

You also can easily represent a budget with a pie chart or display increases in crime with a bar chart. Sometimes doing this helps you see the results of your work more clearly. For example, residents of a city may believe they are paying too much for sewer and water services. They claim that commercial businesses use more water and put a burden on the sewer system but don't pay their fair share. You could obtain the budget figures for revenue from the division and put them on a spreadsheet, as shown in **Figure 4-48.**

Figure 4-48

	A	B
	A11 ▼ =	
	A	**B**
1	**Water and Sewer Division**	**This year**
2		
3	Residential water fees	$ 18,405,222
4	Residential sewer fees	$ 8,324,555
5	Commercial water fees	$ 11,504,302
6	Commercial sewer fees	$ 5,662,131
7	Investment interest	$ 1,445,214
8		
9	**Total**	**$ 45,341,424**

Then you can quickly format them into a pie chart to see what kind of percentage and proportion the amounts have, as in **Figure 4-49,** by choosing that graphic and determining if the residents have a legitimate complaint.

Figure 4-49

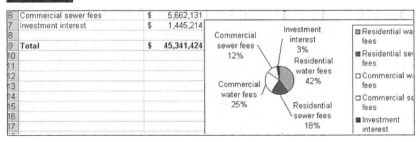

Finally, let's go back to our Pivot Table on Exxon. This time, let's take it one step further. You may have noticed that when you finished your Pivot Table, a Menu Bar of icons popped up. First click in the column labeled "Data" and then click on "Sum of Amount2." This will make your chart simpler. Then click on the Chart Wizard once, and you should have the worksheet shown in **Figure 4-50.**

Figure 4-50

	A	B	C	D	E	F	G	H	I
1	Drop Page Fields Here								
2									
3	Sum of AMOUNT2								
4	PARTY ▼	Total							
5	DEM	23.74%							
6	REP	76.26%							
7	Grand Total	100.00%							
8									
9									
10						PivotTable			
11									
12						PivotTable ▼			
13									
14						COMPANY	AMOL Chart Wizard T...	PARTY

Click on "Pie" and pick the "3D" one, as shown in **Figure 4-51.**

Figure 4-51

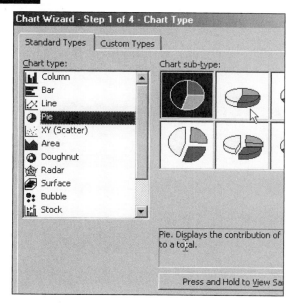

Click on "Next" and you will see a pie chart with the proportion of giving but no percentages, so click on "Data Labels" (see **Figure 4-52**).

Figure 4-52

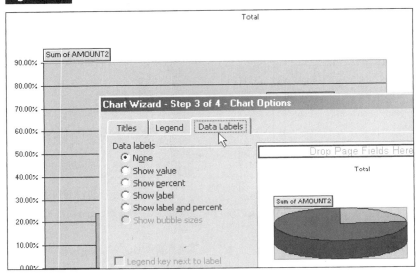

Click on "Show label and percent" as in **Figure 4-53**.

Figure 4-53

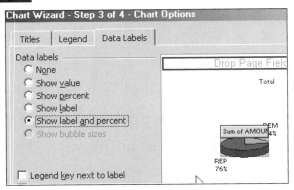

Click on "Next" and then "Finish," and now you have a picture that shows the big difference in giving in **Figure 4-54.**

Figure 4-54

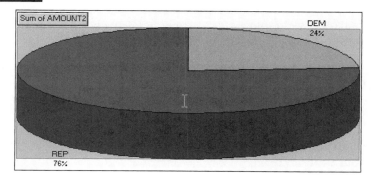

As you can see, spreadsheets can provide detailed analyses and comparisons as well as vivid graphics that make it easier to understand the results. After some practice on spreadsheets, you will be ready to move to database managers, where some of the same analyses can be done but much more quickly and with many more records.

▼ CAR Wars

▼   During the past decade, West Virginia education officials closed one of every five schools in a massive consolidation drive. Parents
▼   and opponents said rural children were forced to ride the bus four hours a day or longer. State officials said most children rode the
▼   bus for only a short time.
      We started with asking a simple question: "How long are chil-
▼   dren's bus rides in West Virginia?" We found that most school districts in 35 rural counties did not keep computerized records, so we obtained the paper records and built our own database in Excel that included when each run started, when it stopped and the time spent in between. Excel was the right tool because we were doing calculations involving the differences in time.
      We found the number of children who rode the bus more than two hours a day doubled during the 1990s. Also, we found that two-thirds of the bus routes carrying elementary schoolchildren exceeded the state guidelines that said children should not be on a bus longer than an hour a day.

Scott Fine and Eric Eyre, The Charleston Gazette

Chapter Checklist

• The use of rates and ratios is a way to fairly compare entities with different populations.

• Spreadsheets allow you to narrow your analysis by filtering in information you want to use.

• Subtotals and Pivot Tables give you a way to total information by categories.

• Charts allow you to visualize information and effectively present your findings.

☛ Your Turn to Practice

1 Find the Bureau of Justice Statistics Web site and download information into a worksheet on crime by year in the United States.

2 Open the file in Excel and calculate the crime rates, using the number of crimes and the populations, for violent crimes and for property crimes.

3 Compare your calculations to those done by the FBI.

4 Do a ratio of property crimes each year to violent crimes each year.

5 Create a pie chart of property crimes and violent crimes from the most recent year.

6 Download campaign finance information from the Center for Responsive Politics on a large company's contributions in the 2000 and 2002 election cycles.

7 Do subtotals and Pivot Tables on which party received the most.

www

For more exercises in downloading and importing, go to
www.ire.org/carbook/chapter4

CHAPTER 5

Database Managers, Part 1

Searching and Summarizing

A team of reporters and editors began culling and analyzing state data from nearly 30,000 crashes over five years along Florida's 382 miles of I-95. In an initial 10-page report, we delivered the news that the number of people killed on the Florida highway had doubled over five years.

— Tony Manolatos, Florida Today

Just how big is the legal gambling industry in Ohio and in the nation, we wondered, and what impact have casinos, multi-state lotteries and other forms of betting in neighboring states had on Ohio? The Ohio Lottery Commission provided an elec-tronic **database** *of sales from stores that sold lottery tickets for the past several years. That made it fairly easy to analyze sales by ZIP codes with Microsoft Access. Using that database and other statistics, The Dispatch was able to estimate that a large chunk of the $9.9 billion in revenue from Ohioans' gam-bling went to neighboring states.*

— Barnet D. Wolf, Columbus Dispatch

Both these stories involved large databases and many categories of information that a spreadsheet would have had a hard time handling. Unlike a spreadsheet, a **database manager** can exam-ine hundreds of thousands of **records** in minutes, organize them into similar groups and compare records in one database with the records in another. Reporters use a database manager to do what they call the "heavy lifting" of data — that is, searching and summarizing large databases.

Many journalists start using a database manager to analyze campaign finance records. These records are public, and they cross over many topics because campaign finance records are a way of tracking access and influence of contributors on issues such as education, health, business and environment.

You can get these records from public agencies or by creating your own database. For years, journalists have conscientiously kept tabs on campaign contributions to politicians. Some have kept lists, some have kept index cards and some have kept the information in their heads. But it can take a lot of time to retrieve that information when it's on paper or in a printout, and even more time to perform calculations on which politician is getting the most contributions and which person is giving the most.

It is ironic that some journalists have persisted in using paper or printouts when (1) the politicians' campaign managers analyze databases, and (2) social scientists and nonprofit watchdog groups use databases to evaluate and criticize the donations.

A database manager helps a journalist search for particular information quickly, do totals for groups of information (summarized data) and combine and make comparisons quickly between different files. A journalist should learn to use a database manager as soon as possible for two technical reasons. A spreadsheet can handle only about 65,000 records, and many databases have more records than that. A database manager can handle a million records. In addition, governments often keep data in relational databases, which contain two or more files that have been joined. So you need to know how to use a database manager in order to analyze that kind of data.

One journalist for The Associated Press decided in the early 1990s that he had had enough and helped develop a campaign finance database in Pennsylvania. "I built my own database with index cards," David Morris said. "Then I decided it was time to move into the 20th century."

The good news for Morris and other journalists who made the change and are now in the 21st century is that electronic federal campaign finance data is easily available, and electronic state campaign finance information is becoming more available.

The Federal Election Commission (FEC) in Washington, D.C., maintains a database on campaign finance information on contributions to federal candidates and to political committees. You can obtain the database online or on **CD-ROM** from the FEC or from nonprofit groups such as the Center for Responsive Politics (**www.opensecrets.org**) or the National Institute for Computer-Assisted Reporting (NICAR). (For instance, the information on Exxon donations in Chapter 4 came from NICAR at **www.campaignfinance.org.**)

Nonetheless, news organizations may still have to create their own databases of local campaign contributions. In addition, journalists generally must create their own databases on campaign expenditures.

By using databases to monitor campaign donations and expenditures, journalists get a good selection of stories to consider and can readily see how data analysis can lead to a story. Furthermore, many editors support doing stories on this particular topic because most consider it a required public service to monitor campaign finance and explain how it influences governmental actions and business.

In addition, a campaign finance database can be used for longer analytical stories while serving as an instant resource for daily stories. After an election is over, a reporter can do a story on how much money the winner received, who gave the most money and from whom the winner received contributions. Then, after the winner takes office and begins to award no-bid contracts, the reporter can quickly determine whether the recipients of the generous contracts had donated money to the winner and how much. A typical headline may read, "Mayor's supporters get lucrative contracts."

Another reason campaign contributions are good fodder for learning database managers is because you initially have to concentrate on only a few columns of information (see **Figure 5-1**).

Figure 5-1

Candidate	Contribution	Contributor

Looking at the 2000 presidential election, we would find these names of contributors to presidential candidates and the amount contributed as in **Figure 5-2.**

Figure 5-2

Candidate	Amount	Contributor
McCain, John S.	500	Dean Petersen
Bush, George W.	1000	A.S. Love
Bush, George W.	1000	A.S. Love
Bradley, Bill	1000	Abraham Margolin
Gore, Al	200	Abram McGull II

In a spreadsheet, the names would appear as they do in **Figure 5-3**. (Note that the contributor names have been split into the last name and the rest of their name. Splitting the names allows you to sort and group by the last name.)

Figure 5-3

	A	B	C	D
1	CANDIDATE	AMOUNT	RESTOFNAME	LASTNAME
2	MCCAIN, JOHN S		500 A. DEAN D. MR.	PETERSEN
3	BUSH, GEORGE W		1000 A. S. MR.	LOVE
4	BUSH, GEORGE W		1000 A. S. MRS.	LOVE
5	BRADLEY, BILL		250 ABRAHAM MR.	MARGOLIN
6	GORE, AL		200 ABRAM MR. II	MCGULL

A major difference in appearance between a spreadsheet and a database manager is that the names of the columns are embedded (see **Figure 5-4**). This means it is not as easy to change the names of the columns. Database managers are a little more formal and rigid than spreadsheets because they deal with much more information.

Figure 5-4

CANDIDATE	AMOUNT	RESTOFNAME	LASTNAME
MCCAIN, JOHN S	500	A. DEAN D. MR.	PETERSEN
BUSH, GEORGE W	1000	A. S. MR.	LOVE
BUSH, GEORGE W	1000	A. S. MRS.	LOVE
BRADLEY, BILL	250	ABRAHAM MR.	MARGOLIN
GORE, AL	200	ABRAM MR. II	MCGULL

Notice that you no longer have letters and numbers to guide you. One difference between spreadsheets and database managers is that information in spreadsheets usually comes to you in some sort of order. In database managers, the information initially may be in a random order because the software assumes you will reorder the information constantly. Furthermore, database manager programs aren't set up to copy formulas, which is why spreadsheets have addresses of numbers and letters.

A database manager is designed to help you look up names quickly. Even if you had 100,000 contributors, you could find in seconds one contributor's name or all the contributors who gave to George W. Bush. You could sort the list alphabetically or by amounts, and you could total the amounts given to each candidate, as shown in **Figure 5-5.**

Figure 5-5

CANDIDATE	SumOfAMOUNT
BUSH, GEORGE W	1358189
BRADLEY, BILL	370238
GORE, AL	222491
MCCAIN, JOHN S	126040
BAUER, GARY L	48052
DOLE, ELIZABETH	46000
BUCHANAN, PATRICK J	34598

Figure 5-5 shows what some journalists call "**summary data.**" It is a summary of many records. This also illustrates the concept of "**grouping.**" *Grouping* means lumping together similar kinds of records. In Chapter 4, the concept was used for subtotaling or in Pivot Tables. Journalists use it when they are going to count the number of records or sum amounts. For many journalists (including myself), grouping was a difficult concept at first, even though we all use it in everyday life.

Many journalists compare grouping in a database manager to playing cards. Because of that, I started handing out playing cards when I taught database managers. In most card games, you are dealt a hand that you have to arrange. You then count the number of cards in each suit, and sometimes you sum up the face card value. Before you do that, however, you do something else with the cards. You group them into suits.

You might be dealt 13 cards: king of hearts, queen of hearts, five of clubs, seven of hearts, five of hearts, ace of diamonds, jack of spades, four of diamonds, eight of spades, six of spades, ten of diamonds, two of hearts and three of diamonds. You divide them into suits: hearts, diamonds,

spades and clubs. You count the cards: You have five hearts, four diamonds, three spades and one club. You sum up the face values (face
cards count 10 and aces 1) and find that you have 34 points in hearts,
18 in diamonds, 24 in spades and 5 in clubs. **Figure 5-6** represents all
this activity.

Figure 5-6

Suit	Count (Number)	Sum (Face Value)
Hearts	5	34
Diamonds	4	18
Spades	3	24
Clubs	1	5

You might do the same activity with coins to see how much money
you have. In either case, a database manager will do exactly this kind of
grouping work for you. Of course, you don't need it for card games, but
you do need it for political contribution games.

Let's go back to our example from the presidential election. If you
want to find out the various totals for the candidates from this sample
database, then you think of the candidates as the equivalent of card
suits. The face value is the contribution.

We'll return to grouping later, but for now we will explore the basic
uses of a database manager. We'll use the database manager known as
Microsoft Access, but remember the concepts are present in all database
managers.

▼ The Query

Unlike a spreadsheet, a database manager is more formal when you want
to use it for analysis. Instead of doing your work on the original data,
the database manager has you create a "**query,**" and then it has you
"run" the query.

Let's take a look at the database of contributions in the 2000 U.S. presidential election. First, we open Access and then under "File" we open a
database called "Prez Race." When we open that, we will find a screen in
which we have a Table (which is like an individual file) called "Prez." See
Figure 5-7.

Figure 5-7

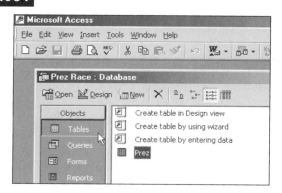

By double-clicking on "Prez" we can see our data as in **Figure 5-8.**

Figure 5-8

	CANDIDATE	AMOUNT	RESTOFNAME	LASTNAME
▶	DOLE, ELIZABETH	1000	PETER M. MR.	ABEL
	GORE, AL	1000	ALEX MR.	ABOUSSIE
	GORE, AL	1000	ALICE MRS.	ABOUSSIE
	GORE, AL	500	ALICIA L. MS.	ABOUSSIE
	GORE, AL	500	JILL M. MS.	ABOUSSIE
	GORE, AL	1000	JOYCE MS.	ABOUSSIE
	GORE, AL	1000	LINDA M. MRS.	ABOUSSIE
	MCCAIN, JOHN S	500	ROBERT MR.	ACKERBURG

Closing the window, by clicking in the "X" in the top right-hand corner, we return to the previous screen. We have seen the data, but now we want to analyze it. To do that, we click on "Queries" and get the screen shown in **Figure 5-9,** where we double-click on "Create query in Design view." This means that we are going to fill in a form to ask a question.

Figure 5-9

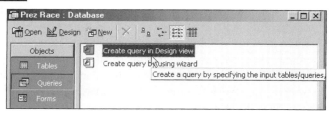

After double-clicking, we are asked what table (file) we want to look at, and we click on "Add" as in **Figure 5-10.**

Figure 5-10

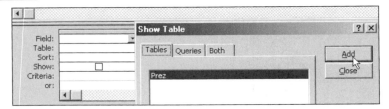

After we click on "Add," we see in **Figure 5-11** that a box has appeared in the upper window, and in that box are the names of the columns, which are called **"fields"** in database managers. We close the lower window, and now we are ready to begin our analysis.

Figure 5-11

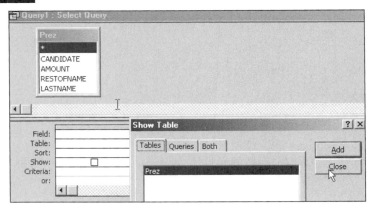

▼ Selecting and Searching

The first strength of a database manager is speedy **searches.** If you want to find a name, you tell the database manager that you want to look for all the information on that particular name.

First, you select the columns you want to use. The concept of "**select**" allows you to cull through the columns in a database. Often, government databases have 30 or more columns of information. Selection of the fields is important because it clears away distractions. Furthermore, many journalists' analyses eventually involve only three or four fields. As in **Figure 5-12,** you need to select only three fields — Restofname, Lastname, Amount — to see who gave how much. You do this by double-clicking on each field name in the upper window, and the field name appears in successive columns in the lower window.

Figure 5-12

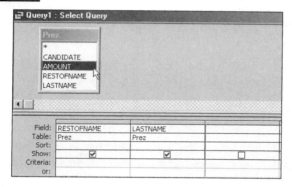

Make sure that a checkmark appears in the box on the "Show" line so that the information in that field will appear in the answer. Now go to the Menu Bar and click on the exclamation sign (!) to "run" the query, as shown in **Figure 5-13.**

Figure 5-13

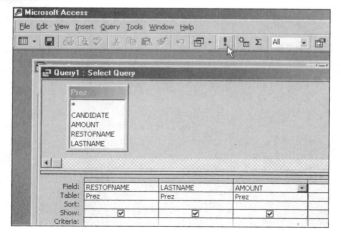

As a result, we get only the three fields we chose, as shown in **Figure 5-14.**

Figure 5-14

RESTOFNAME	LASTNAME	AMOUNT
PETER M. MR.	ABEL	1000
ALEX MR.	ABOUSSIE	1000
ALICE MRS.	ABOUSSIE	1000
▶ ALICIA L. MS.	ABOUSSIE	500
JILL M. MS.	ABOUSSIE	500
JOYCE MS.	ABOUSSIE	1000
LINDA M. MRS.	ABOUSSIE	1000
ROBERT MR.	ACKERBURG	500
ROBERT MR.	ACKERBURG	500
MILLY MRS.	ACUFF	200
LEANNE	ADAMS	200

Query1 : Select Query

We have not lost any of the other information in the Table called "Prez," but we have simply selected three fields temporarily to show in our answer. This "vertical" cut of the information shows us how easy it is to include some information and exclude other information. If we don't save this result, it will simply disappear when we return to the original information.

To return to our query form, we just hit the "Design View" symbol in the left-hand top corner, as shown in **Figure 5-15.**

Figure 5-15

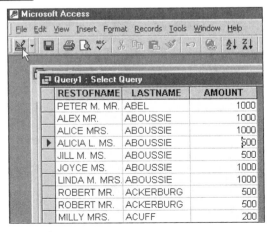

▼ Criteria and Filtering

After looking at the fields, you might want to look just at the contributors who gave more than $500. The idea is the same as in Chapter 4, where you used the "Filter" in Excel to limit the information you received. After returning to your query form, click on the "Criteria" line under "Amount" and type ">500," as shown in **Figure 5-16.**

Figure 5-16

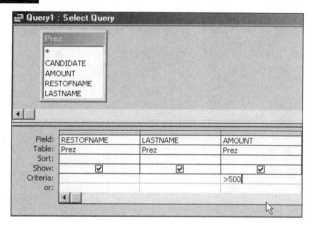

Now run the query, and your answer appears as in **Figure 5-17,** showing only those who gave more than $500. (A helpful hint: When you type a number such as 1000, do not put in any commas, or the program may not read it correctly.)

Figure 5-17

RESTOFNAME	LASTNAME	AMOUNT
PETER M. MR.	ABEL	1000
ALEX MR.	ABOUSSIE	1000
ALICE MRS.	ABOUSSIE	1000
JOYCE MS.	ABOUSSIE	1000
LINDA M. MRS.	ABOUSSIE	1000
STEPHEN S III	ADAMS	1000
LARRY MR. JR	AGNEW	750
DON H	ALEXANDER	1000
DON H. MR.	ALEXANDER	1000
BARBARA L. M	ALLEN	2000

▼ Sorting

If you want to sort the contributions from highest to lowest, you use the same principle as in the spreadsheet. Click the icon to return to the query form and choose the "Amount" field. Identify the sorting order as "descending," as shown in **Figure 5-18.**

Figure 5-18

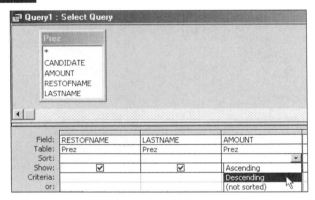

After you run the query, you will see that the answer is now sorted by highest amount to lowest, as shown in **Figure 5-19.**

Figure 5-19

RESTOFNAME	LASTNAME	AMOUNT
JAMES N	MILLS	20000
DONALD J	HALL	20000
ROY	PFAUTCH	15000
WILLIAM O III	DEWITT	12500
CAMILLA T	BRAUER	10000
ANDREW N	BAUR	10000
VALERIE D. MS.	HEITSHUSEN	4092
DENNIS M. MR.	JONES	2000
DAVID	LIMBAUGH	2000

▼ Criteria and Wildcards

Database managers allow you to single out one individual by using filters. The filters may be under "Criteria" or they may be in "where" statements (which we will cover later) such as "where Lastname = "Balsiger"."

But database managers also have another powerful filtering function called "like." "Like" lets you choose a name using only a few letters in the name. Because data entry can be an error-prone endeavor, names are often spelled in several different ways in governmental databases. Using "like" is one way to get around the problem.

As shown in **Figure 5-20,** you can look for all the Balsigers by using "like" and something known as a wildcard. In the Access database manager, the wildcard is an asterisk (*). In others, it may be a percent sign (%) or two periods (..). In any case, like a joker in a deck of cards it can stand for anything; the wildcard after "bal" stands for all the numbers or letters that might follow the letters "bal". (Lower- or uppercase doesn't matter.)

In the **Figure 5-20,** you type in "bal*" under the "Lastname" field and run the query.

Figure 5-20

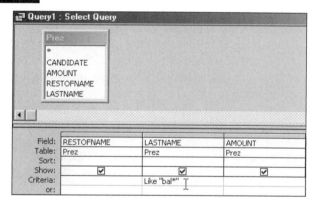

Your query result picks up every name that begins with "Bal," ensuring that you didn't miss any misspellings in the table (see **Figure 5-21**).

Figure 5-21

RESTOFNAME	LASTNAME	AMOUNT
EDWARD MR.	BALMES	1000
CRAIG MR.	BALSIGER	600
CRAIG MR.	BALSIGER	200
CRAIG MR.	BALSIGER	200
JANICE MRS.	BALZER	300
JANICE MRS.	BALZER	300
JANICE MRS.	BALZER	200

▼ Boolean Logic: And, Or, Not

Another strength of database managers is that the search can incorporate two or more criteria. To do that, you use the logic we spoke about in Chapter 2: Boolean logic. Some modern librarians call it "a life skill." It is also a routine way of doing online searches.

Boolean logic uses the words *and, or* and *not*. Those three little words are incredibly powerful. You might want to search for everyone who gave more than $500 to Bush or Gore. Boolean logic treats the search in this way: Give me everyone who donated to Gore **"or"** Bush **"and"** who gave more than $500.

Access and other user-friendly database managers actually are making it easy to do Boolean logic. In most searches online, or in more sophisticated databases, you would write "where (candidate = "Bush" or candidate = "Gore") and contribution >500." (We will address that in Chapter 6.)

You must pay attention to your **"ors"** and **"ands"** and be very careful with **"nots."** If you are choosing items in the same field, you don't write "where city = "New York" **and** city = "Los Angeles."" How can you be in two places at once? In fact, with that question, you are nowhere at all.

Also as a general rule, if you are choosing items in the same field, put parentheses around them. For example, if you are looking for all the murderers in New York City or Los Angeles, you would write "city = ("New York" or "Los Angeles") and crime = "murderers."" If you write "city = "New York" or city = "Los Angeles" and crime = "murderers,"" you would probably get all the criminals in New York City and all the murderers in Los Angeles.

"Not" is particularly handy when you want to exclude a set of information. If you are analyzing an election in Wisconsin and you wanted to look at only out-of-state contributors, you would use a "not." You would write a query that said "where state = **not** "Wisconsin.""

Let's return to our table on the presidential contributions and give it a try with a query form by looking for everyone who gave more than $500 to Bush. As shown in **Figure 5-22,** we will double-click on "Candidate" to add that field, use a wildcard, type "Bush*" on the criteria line under the Field "Candidate" and type ">500" under the Field "Amount."

Figure 5-22

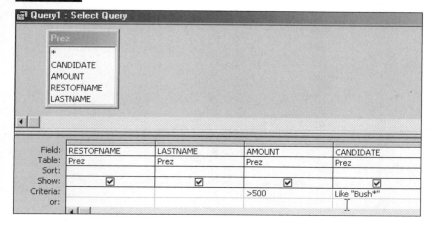

This translates to wanting to see the name of everyone who gave to Bush **and** who gave more than $500 to Bush. If we run this query, we get the results shown in **Figure 5-23.**

Figure 5-23

RESTOFNAME	LASTNAME	AMOUNT	CANDIDATE
STEPHEN S III	ADAMS	1000	BUSH, GEORGE W
DON H	ALEXANDER	1000	BUSH, GEORGE W
DON H. MR.	ALEXANDER	1000	BUSH, GEORGE W
BARBARA L. MR.	ALLEN	2000	BUSH, GEORGE W
C. ROBERT MR.	ALLEN	1000	BUSH, GEORGE W
CHERYL M	ALLEN	1000	BUSH, GEORGE W
JOEL	ALLEN	1000	BUSH, GEORGE W
KRISTI L	ALLEN	1000	BUSH, GEORGE W
RICHARD C	ALLEN	1000	BUSH, GEORGE W

If you wanted to see everyone who gave $500 to Bush or Gore, you would place Bush and Gore on the same line using **"or,"** as shown in **Figure 5-24,** and use the wildcard.

Figure 5-24

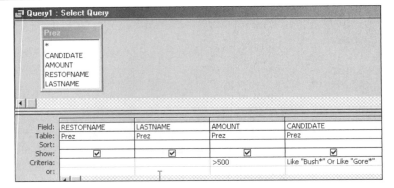

Running the query will get you the result shown in **Figure 5-25**; you can see that you get all contributions above $500 that went to either Bush or Gore.

Figure 5-25

RESTOFNAME	LASTNAME	AMOUNT	CANDIDATE
ALEX MR.	ABOUSSIE	1000	GORE, AL
ALICE MRS.	ABOUSSIE	1000	GORE, AL
JOYCE MS.	ABOUSSIE	1000	GORE, AL
LINDA M. MRS.	ABOUSSIE	1000	GORE, AL
STEPHEN S III	ADAMS	1000	BUSH, GEORGE W
DON H	ALEXANDER	1000	BUSH, GEORGE W
DON H. MR.	ALEXANDER	1000	BUSH, GEORGE W
BARBARA L. MR.	ALLEN	2000	BUSH, GEORGE W
C. ROBERT MR.	ALLEN	1000	BUSH, GEORGE W

▼ Grouping

Once you have selected your fields, set your criteria and then sorted, you still might want to know which candidate received the most money. This is where the idea of grouping, or as it is known in database parlance "Group By," comes in.

"Group By" is the way to quickly summarize data to look for patterns, trends, outliers and even errors in the data. This is one of the sharpest tools that a journalist can use.

First, we decide what category (field) we want to "Group By" and what field we want to add up. In this example, we want to total the "amount" for each "candidate." We can start a new query in our query form by clicking on "Clear Grid" in the Menu Bar under "Edit," as shown in **Figure 5-26.**

Figure 5-26

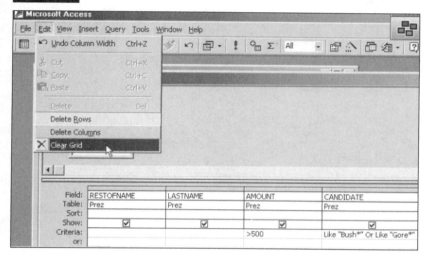

Now we double-click on "Candidate" and on "Amount" to start our new query, as shown in **Figure 5-27.**

Figure 5-27

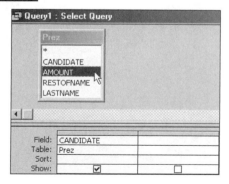

This means we will "Group By" the field "Candidate." We will use the amount field, of course, to add the contributions. To total the amount for each candidate, we have to hit the "Total" button in the Menu Bar that will add a line to the lower window, where we can tell the software to add the contributions, as shown in **Figure 5-28.**

Figure 5-28

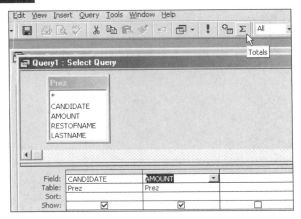

After clicking on "Totals," we will see the new line called "Total" in the lower window as in **Figure 5-29.** Note how "Group By" shows up on that line under the two fields.

Figure 5-29

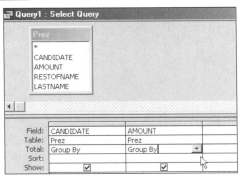

We want to "Group By" the "Candidate" names — that is, divide up the contributions for each candidate. But we don't want to group the amounts; we want to "sum" them as we did when we were doing

subtotals and Pivot Tables in Chapter 4. So we click on the arrow next to
"Group By" under "Amount" and select "Sum," as shown in **Figure 5-30.**

Figure 5-30

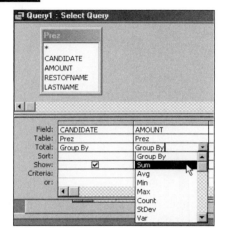

After choosing "Sum," we also can choose to sort our results in
descending order by the total amounts so that we will see which candidate received the most money (see **Figure 5-31**).

Figure 5-31

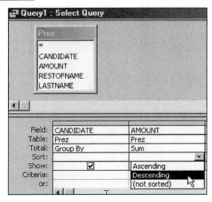

Run the query, and there is your answer that totals contributions by
candidate (see **Figure 5-32**). For a database manager, it doesn't matter

whether you were looking at 50 records or 500,000 records. It groups, adds and sorts.

Figure 5-32

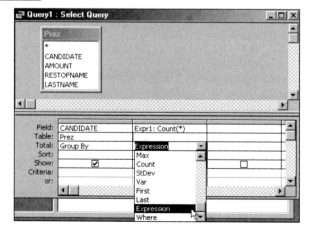

You also can count the total number of contributions by using "Group By." It's a bit trickier because the best way to count items in a table is to type "Count (*)" in the field name and choose "Expression" instead of "Group By," as shown in **Figure 5-33.** By using this method, you will count not only the fields filled in, but also the blank fields. This is usually an important analysis to do.

Figure 5-33

After you type in "Count (*)" and choose "Expression," you can then sort in descending order, as shown in **Figure 5-34.**

Figure 5-34

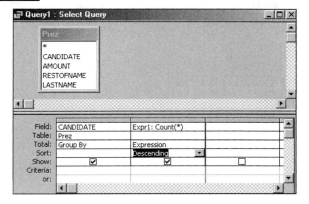

When you run the query, you will get a count of the total number of contributions made to each candidate as in **Figure 5-35.**

Figure 5-35

CANDIDATE	Expr1
BUSH, GEORGE W	1820
BRADLEY, BILL	602
GORE, AL	354
MCCAIN, JOHN S	263
BAUER, GARY L	152
BUCHANAN, PATRICK J	109
DOLE, ELIZABETH	90
KEYES, ALAN L	81
FORBES, STEVE	77
BROWNE, HARRY	40
LAROUCHE, LYNDON H J	40
HAGELIN, JOHN SAMUEL	31
QUAYLE, DAN	24

Record: 17 of 20

Just to review how similar the analysis between a spreadsheet and a database manager can be, let's look at the same Exxon file that we used in Chapter 4. We could do what we did with subtotals, by building this query as in **Figure 5-36,** to show how much each party received from the corporation.

Figure 5-36

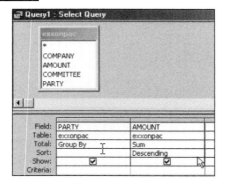

And in **Figure 5-37,** we see the same result done much more quickly and simply.

Figure 5-37

PARTY	SumOfAMOUN
REP	$530,000.00
DEM	$165,000.00

Once you feel comfortable with these different queries, you will use a query that has been the basis for many computer-assisted reporting stories. You obtain information, you divide the information into groups, you count or sum parts of the information by groups and you sort your results from highest to lowest. (In the midst of the query, you may filter in or filter out information with "where" statements.)

Once you know the formula, you can enter many different kinds of information. You could look at a prison population, divide it into races and then count the number to find the percentage of minorities and whites in prison. You could then compare it to the percentage of minorities in the community.

You could look at blighted properties in your city, divide the information into neighborhoods and then count the number of blighted properties in each neighborhood. You could take thousands of records of federal contracts in your state, divide the information by communities in which work is being done, sum the amounts of the contracts and then get an idea of the federal contracts' economic importance to those communities. You could look at records of toxic chemical emissions into the environment by manufacturers, divide the information by communities, sum the emissions by communities and then find out which community has the most toxic releases. Much of the information you collect can be examined in this way.

With this basic information, you start your traditional reporting — interviews and site visits — at an advanced level. With the analysis of the relevant databases, you already have seen trends and patterns, seen the unusual — the "outliers" — and are already thinking of follow-up questions to the data. It is as though a tipster or an inside source called you on the phone and told you what you should be looking at. In this case, however, the tipster is not a person, it's a database.

In the next chapter, we will look at more advanced ways of doing this work. The upcoming skills will show you how to compare tables to come up with unique stories and will give you even more control in analyzing data. For more exercises in downloading and importing, go to **www.ire.org/carbook/chapter2.**

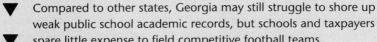

▼ CAR Wars

▼ Compared to other states, Georgia may still struggle to shore up weak public school academic records, but schools and taxpayers
▼ spare little expense to field competitive football teams.
    Teaming with David Milliron, the newspaper's director of
▼ computer-assisted reporting, we built a comprehensive database of the nearly 2,400 high school football coaches and assistant coaches
▼ in the state. The database was built in Microsoft Excel and analyzed in Microsoft Access.
    Gathering the salary and teaching assignment information from 312 public schools proved to be a daily battle. Initially, districts refused to comply or said it would cost hundreds of dollars to produce the information, but eventually we got the data for the salaries for teachers and coaches. By having the database, we were able to group and total salaries and search quickly for individual information.
    Once we had done our analysis and our reporting, we published stories questioning whether education is being compromised for

> playing football games. We found nearly $80 million in state tax dollars spent for coaches' salaries in one year, and head football coaches making 55 percent more than the average for academic teachers.
>
> **Mike Fish,** The Atlanta Journal-Constitution

 Chapter Checklist

- Database managers handle large numbers of records and allow you to organize the data the way you want.

- Database managers can do speedy searches for particular information.

- Database managers allow you to filter information easily.

- Database managers can quickly create summary data by "grouping" categories of information and allowing you to total the numbers or items in those groups.

 Your Turn to Practice

1 Get a database of registered gun dealers in your state from the Bureau of Tobacco, Alcohol, and Firearms from the National Institute for Computer-Assisted Reporting.

2 Do a query searching for your city.

3 Do a query in which you group and count the gun dealers in each city in your state. Sort the records from highest to lowest number of gun dealers.

4 Do a query in which you group and count gun dealers by ZIP code in your city and the largest city in the state. Sort the records from highest to lowest number of gun dealers.

www

For more exercises in downloading and importing, go to
www.ire.org/carbook/chapter5

▷ CHAPTER **6**

Database Managers, Part 2

Matchmaking and Advanced Queries

> *Taking two large databases, one of people licensed to work as aides in home health care and one of criminals, The Star-Ledger, based in Newark, New Jersey, found more than 100 recently convicted criminals certified to work unsupervised in the homes of the most vulnerable residents of the state. The matching of criminal identities with aides' identities helped reveal lax state policies and also helped protect those needing assistance at home.*
>
> **— Robert Gebeloff, The Star-Ledger**

$\mathbf{A}$s you can see from this public service story, one of most valuable uses of a database manager is matching information in one file to information in another file. This chapter covers **relational databases,** in which files, known as tables, are intentionally linked to one another. Information is separated into "linked" tables because it organizes the information and cuts back on the amount of time it takes to do data entry.

But many reporters now use database managers to do enterprising comparisons of files never created to be linked together — as Robert Gebeloff did in the story at the beginning of this chapter.

For decades, reporters have looked at relationships between people and agencies in a slower, paper-laden way. In campaign finance, they have done rudimentary matching of businesses' contributions to a candidate and the government contract that those businesses received after the candidate won election. Quite often, they did the matching on index cards or notebook paper.

Other reporters looked at reams of paper of criminal incidents and then looked at local police department decisions on deploying its patrol officers. Others went through environmental agency files on waste dumps and their locations and then looked at printouts of U.S. Census information to see whether the dumps were being placed in low-income areas that had little political clout.

Utilizing a database manager and relational databases to do these same tasks is simply using a better, faster way of doing the traditional kind of reporting. In the 21st century, information about you is kept in many relational databases. (That's how marketing people find you to make those annoying phone calls, send you spam or bury you in direct mail.)

If you have a job at a large business or with a government agency, the organization probably keeps your personal information, such as your name and place of residence, in a table as part of a relational database (see **Figure 6-1**). **Figure 6-1** is also a record layout of the table that we will discuss in later chapters.

Figure 6-1

Employee : Table

Field Name	Data Type
Employee Id	Text
Lastname	Text
Firstname	Text
Street	Text
Town	Text
Zip	Text

Figure 6-2 shows another table that is a list of the paychecks you received and the date on which you received them — another record layout.

Figure 6-2

Employee Pay : Table

Field Name	Data Type
Employee ID	Text
Pay	Number
Date	Date/Time

Note that each field has an employee ID and that only an ID, not a name, appears in the salary table. The ID field is known as a key field. It's the field that links the two tables together, as shown in **Figure 6-3.** You link tables together using a query.

Figure 6-3

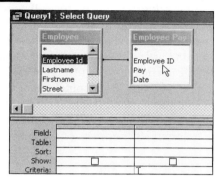

By linking the two tables, you can match each employee's name with payroll information. This saves space because you don't have to type all the information about the employee each time you enter information about payroll. The tables also organize information efficiently into subjects. Database managers can automatically create key fields of IDs (as we will discuss in Chapter 7) or can use an already existing ID.

What's the most universal key field in the United States? The Social Security number. If you have someone's Social Security number, you can link tables and tables of information together.

But how do you create a link? You tell the database manager that when the **ID number** in a record in the employee table equals the ID number in employee payroll, then the information should be matched, creating a longer record. In many database managers this is much easier to do than it used to be. In Microsoft Access, you can actually draw a line from one table to another by clicking on the employee ID field and then dragging the cursor onto the ID in the salary table.

In other database managers, the software automatically guesses the connection for you. You can also write a "where" statement in a universal programming language known as Structured Query Language (**SQL**). The statement says to link the two files together (as in **Figure 6-3,** where the Employee ID in the Employee table = the Employee ID in the

Employee Pay table). Later in this chapter we will do some basic SQL statements because SQL is a straightforward programming language that every good database manager has. In addition, SQL makes you think clearly about the questions you are asking and, once mastered, allows you to write queries faster.

You might wonder why you should care about an employee relational database. Well, many governmental databases you ask for will be relational, especially if they contain employee information. You need to know what bureaucrats mean when they say it's a relational database. You also must know that you need to ask what the key field (or fields) is.

As you learned in Chapter 5, one of the most popular databases is from the Federal Election Commission (FEC). If you obtain data from the FEC, you will get a candidates table, a political action committee contribution table, an individual contributor table and a political committee table. You link those tables by the ID numbers of committees and candidates.

To find information about a candidate, you would go to the "candidates" table. In that table, you would find the ID numbers for the committees set up by the candidate to receive the contributions. To find information about the committees, you would link the candidates table to the political committee table through the ID numbers. To determine which individuals contributed to the candidate, you would link the committee table to the individual contributor table by the committee ID that is present in both tables. It's not unlike building bridges between islands of information.

For our immediate purposes, we can look at some slightly simplified FEC data that NICAR created on Missouri residents who contributed to the 2000 presidential election. The table for the last chapter, "Prez," was actually created by linking two FEC tables together. One table contained information on contributors, and one contained information on the candidates. In this chapter we will work with the two tables both separately and together.

To get those two tables, you click on the "Create a Query" button and go to "Design View." Instead of just adding one table to the upper window, you add both tables one at a time, as shown in **Figure 6-4.** Note that the candidate table, MOCANDS, has been added, and now we are adding the contributors in MOGIVE.

Figure 6-4

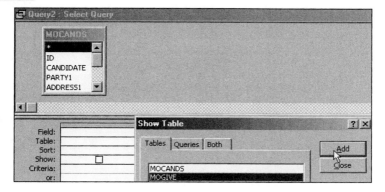

After adding both tables, we click our cursor on "ID" in "MOCANDS" and drag it to "CAND_ID" in "MOGIVE" to link the tables (see **Figure 6-5**).

Figure 6-5

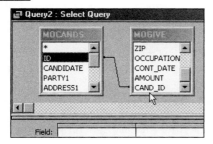

Now that we have correctly linked the tables, we can treat the two tables as one and choose fields from each, as shown in **Figure 6-6.**

Figure 6-6

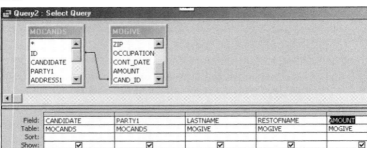

Run the query, and you will get the fields from both tables as in **Figure 6-7.**

Figure 6-7

CANDIDATE	PARTY1	LASTNAME	RESTOFNAME	AMOUNT
DOLE, ELIZABETH	REP	ABEL	PETER M. MR.	1000
DOLE, ELIZABETH	REP	ALLEN	STEWART W. I	200
DOLE, ELIZABETH	REP	ANGELL	WILEY D. MR.	250
DOLE, ELIZABETH	REP	BACKERMAN	MILLARD	-1000
DOLE, ELIZABETH	REP	BACKERMAN	MILLARD MR.	1000
DOLE, ELIZABETH	REP	BEALE	CYNTHIA	-150
DOLE, ELIZABETH	REP	BEHNKE	BARRY L. MR.	250

▼ Enterprise Matchmaking

The previous example is a case of "intentional" matching, or joining of tables. But journalists can do extraordinary work by linking tables that weren't created to be linked. In this way, journalists can cross the borders between agencies, professions and fiefdoms. For more than a decade, journalists have used **enterprise matchmaking** to ferret out criminals in school systems, nursing homes or home health care programs. Other examples include seeing if lottery sales are primarily in low-income areas or if legislators who set taxes are actually paying their own. Journalists seeking dead voters have linked street addresses or names of voters with names on death certificates. The possibilities are limited only by the imagination of the journalist and the availability of the data.

Journalists don't always have the Social Security number and therefore must be a bit more creative. When a relationship is not intended, they have to come up with one or more key fields. Several newspapers have found criminals working in school classrooms despite rules that prohibit felons — in particular, child molesters — from being hired. The general method has been one of linking court or prison records to employee records by matching first name to first name, last name to last name and date of birth to date of birth.

In **Figure 6-8,** for example, you have teachers. (None of these names represent real people.)

Figure 6-8

Lastname	Firstname	Date of Birth	Date of Hire	School
Smith	Joseph	11/1/1965	1/10/1990	Nixon
Barry	Donald	10/12/1955	8/3/1991	Kennedy
Neff	Arnold	4/2/1959	8/3/1991	Jefferson
Harwood	Mary	3/14/1969	8/3/1991	Jefferson
Atwater	Gerald	2/1/1953	9/5/1991	Madison

In **Figure 6-9,** you have criminals.

Figure 6-9

Lastname	Firstname	Date of Birth	Charge
Barry	Donald	10/12/1955	Child molest
Smith	Walter	2/14/1957	Child molest
Walker	Edward	5/10/1961	Child molest
Nadell	Samuel	12/4/1962	Rape
Harwood	Mary	3/14/1969	Assault

You link them by looking at both tables at once and linking them by several fields, since you don't have a key field such as a Social Security number. To link, you click and drag each similar field (see **Figure 6-10**).

Figure 6-10

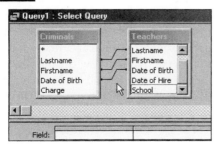

Choose the fields Lastname, Firstname, School and Date of Birth from the Teachers table, and Date of Birth and Charge from the Criminals table, as in **Figure 6-11.**

Figure 6-11

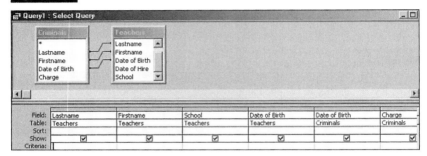

Run the query, and the result looks like **Figure 6-12,** showing the potential matches between teachers and criminals.

Figure 6-12

Lastname	Firstname	School	Teachers.Date	Criminals.Date	Charge
Barry	Donald	Kennedy	10/12/1955	10/12/1955	Child molest
Harwood	Mary	Jefferson	3/14/1969	3/14/1969	Assault

Of course, the reporting would have just begun. You need to double-check your information, use other documents to verify that the teacher and criminal are the same person and then prepare to do the difficult interviews with the employees and the school system officials.

But if you have a list of foster parents in your state and a list of criminal records, a good number of **matches** (or "hits," as they are known) leads to good public service journalism that protects the weak or vulnerable. The Charlotte Observer in North Carolina produced such a story. In Massachusetts, Brad Goldstein, formerly of the Lawrence Eagle-Tribune, found welfare recipients in jail by matching the names of recipients with a list of prison inmates. After Hurricane Andrew ravaged Florida, Steve Doig of The Miami Herald matched building inspection records with wind velocities in the same areas. If the wind was low and the damage was high, then he knew there probably was a problem with construction standards in that area. More recently, the Atlanta Journal-Constitution discovered that teachers who were convicted felons had escaped scrutiny when being hired. Other reporters have even compared parking tickets and weather conditions to show that tickets are seldom given out when the weather is bad.

The matchmaking possibilities are limited only by the validity of the comparison. You need to be sure of the accuracy of each match, and that will require more work. You must review your work and then, as just mentioned, find ways through other documents and interviews to ensure that the matches are accurate and your story is solid.

▼ Structured Query Language

Once you have mastered the basics of using the visual "query by example" tool of database managers, you are ready to learn the basics of Structured Query Language (SQL), the common programming language for doing analysis in most database managers.

The name may sound imposing, but many working journalists believe that SQL gives them much flexibility and control over their queries and also makes them think through their analyses more carefully.

SQL has six fundamental commands.

- **SELECT** is a way to choose the fields (columns) of information you want. You can also use it to calculate differences in numeric fields or create new fields.
- **FROM** chooses which table or tables to use.
- **WHERE** allows you to filter the records you want to see based on certain criteria.
- **GROUP BY** is a way of summarizing information whenever you do math such as adding up (summing) amounts or counting the number of times something occurs. You must use it carefully in conjunction with the **SELECT statement.** You generally would not use GROUP BY unless you want to total.
- **HAVING** allows you to limit the number of records in your answer if you have summarized (using GROUP BY) the records.
- **ORDER BY** is sorting. It lets you sort your answer from highest to lowest by a particular field just as you did in a spreadsheet or in the previous chapter in Access.

Using SQL in Microsoft Access

To use SQL in Microsoft Access, you can begin as you did when asking questions in the previous chapter. Proceed as though you were going to create a new query in the Prez database we have been using, and add the table "Prez," as shown in **Figure 6-13.**

Figure 6-13

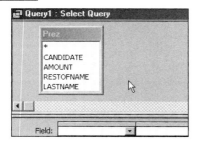

Now go to the left-hand corner to the Design View icon, click on the small arrow next to it and choose "SQL View," as shown in **Figure 6-14.**

Figure 6-14

When you click on "SQL View," you are sent to a screen where the program has already started an SQL query for you (see **Figure 6-15**).

Figure 6-15

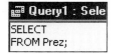

Note that you have "SELECT" and "FROM," which every SQL query must have. Why? Because you cannot ask a question and expect an answer unless you are using a table and choosing fields to show. "SELECT" says which fields will be chosen, and "FROM" says which table from which you will choose those fields.

In this case, let's choose all the fields to show using a wildcard — "*" — as in **Figure 6-16.** (The semicolon at the end tells the program that the line is the end of the whole query.)

Figure 6-16

Run the query by clicking on the exclamation mark, and you get the result in **Figure 6-17** — the contributors to each candidate and the amount they contributed.

Figure 6-17

CANDIDATE	AMOUNT	RESTOFNAME	LASTNAME
DOLE, ELIZABETH	1000	PETER M. MR.	ABEL
GORE, AL	1000	ALEX MR.	ABOUSSIE
GORE, AL	1000	ALICE MRS.	ABOUSSIE
GORE, AL	500	ALICIA L. MS.	ABOUSSIE
GORE, AL	500	JILL M. MS.	ABOUSSIE
GORE, AL	1000	JOYCE MS.	ABOUSSIE
GORE, AL	1000	LINDA M. MRS.	ABOUSSIE
MCCAIN, JOHN S	500	ROBERT MR.	ACKERBURG

Click on the Design View icon and return to "SQL View." This time select just two fields — "Amount" and "Candidate" — in that sequence as in **Figure 6-18.**

Figure 6-18

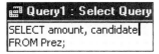

Run that query, and you see how you can choose just two fields and place them in any order you want to, as shown in **Figure 6-19.**

Figure 6-19

AMOUNT	CANDIDATE
1000	DOLE, ELIZABETH
1000	GORE, AL
1000	GORE, AL
500	GORE, AL
500	GORE, AL
1000	GORE, AL
1000	GORE, AL
500	MCCAIN, JOHN S

Return to "SQL View," and this time let's use the "where" statement to limit our result to contributors to Gore (see **Figure 6-20**). Note that we use the word "like" as we did in Chapter 5 and the "*" wildcard. We also surround the word *Gore* in double quotation marks. Use quotation marks whenever the field contains text information. Text means any combination of letters and numbers.

Figure 6-20

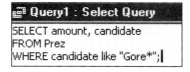

Run the query, and you will see in **Figure 6-21** that you have chosen only Gore contributors.

Figure 6-21

amount	candidate
1000	GORE, AL
1000	GORE, AL
500	GORE, AL
500	GORE, AL
1000	GORE, AL

Query1 : Select Query

Let's return to "SQL View" and see how easy it is to total how much Gore received. We delete "candidate" in the SELECT statement and type "sum" and put "amount" in parentheses, just as we did when using Excel (see **Figure 6-22**).

Figure 6-22

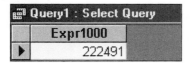

Query1 : Select Query

```
SELECT sum (amount)
FROM Prez
WHERE candidate like "Gore*";
```

Run the query, and you see that you get one number, which is the total given to Gore, as shown in **Figure 6-23.** The total is given the field name of an expression, but you can change the name of the field later if you want.

Figure 6-23

Query1 : Select Query

Expr1000
▶ 222491

It would be logical to want to see how much each candidate received, and that is where we use GROUP BY. Remember that GROUP BY divides the records in the table into groups of similar categories, after which you can count or sum each group — just like subtotals.

Returning to "SQL View," we start a new query. We know that we want the candidates' names and we want the amount totaled for each candidate. That means we want two fields in our answer. So we type "SELECT candidate, sum (amount)."

We know our table is named "Prez," so we type "FROM Prez" on our second line. We are not limiting the contributions to any candidate, so we know we don't need a **WHERE statement.**

We do know we are going to GROUP BY contributions by candidate, so that means we type "GROUP BY candidate." With just a few words, we are finished, and we end with a semicolon. Our query should now look like the one in **Figure 6-24.**

Figure 6-24

```
🖳 Query1 : Select Query
SELECT candidate, sum (amount)
FROM Prez
GROUP BY candidate;
```

Run the query, and you have the total given to each candidate, as shown in **Figure 6-25.**

Figure 6-25

candidate	Expr1001
ALEXANDER, ANDREW L	3000
BAUER, GARY L	48052
BRADLEY, BILL	370238
BROWNE, HARRY	19775
BUCHANAN, PATRICK J	34598
BUSH, GEORGE W	1358189
DOLE, ELIZABETH	46000
FORBES, STEVE	27520
GORE, AL	222491
HAGELIN, JOHN SAMUEL	8700
HATCH, ORRIN GRANT	5750

The result is automatically sorted in alphabetical order of the candidates' names. But we usually want to see who got the most at the top, which means we need to sort our results in descending order.

We return to our query and type a new line with ORDER BY, which essentially means sort. But we can use a shortcut. Since the amount is in the second column (the 2 column), we need only type "ORDER BY 2 desc," with "desc" standing for descending, as in **Figure 6-26.** Don't forget to put the semicolon only at the end of the query.

Figure 6-26

```
🗱 Query1 : Select Query
SELECT candidate, sum (amount)
FROM Prez
GROUP BY candidate
ORDER BY 2 desc;|
```

When you run the query, you see the new order in which the information is sorted (see **Figure 6-27**).

Figure 6-27

🗱 Query1 : Select Query	
candidate	Expr1001
▶ BUSH, GEORGE W	1358189
BRADLEY, BILL	370238
GORE, AL	222491
MCCAIN, JOHN S	126040
BAUER, GARY L	48052
DOLE, ELIZABETH	46000
BUCHANAN, PATRICK J	34598
FORBES, STEVE	27520
KEYES, ALAN L	24848
BROWNE, HARRY	19775
NADER, RALPH	16292
LAROUCHE, LYNDON H .	13035

After examining your answer, you may want to limit the number of candidates to those who received more than $50,000. You might also want to see how many contributions were given in addition to the amount. Both are easy to do in SQL.

In the query, insert a HAVING statement by typing "HAVING sum(amount) > 50000." HAVING is like the WHERE statement except that HAVING is only used as a criterion after you have GROUPED BY.

Then go to the SELECT statement and add a comma after "sum(amount)" and then type "count(*)" at the end of the line. (You don't need a space between "sum" and "(amount)" or "count(*)".) This tells the program to count the number of contributions to each candidate. Your query should look like **Figure 6-28.**

Figure 6-28

```
Query1 : Select Query
SELECT candidate, sum (amount), count (*)
FROM Prez
GROUP BY candidate
HAVING sum(amount) > 50000
ORDER BY 2 desc;
```

After running the query, you should get a highly defined answer that is usable in newspaper, on air or on the Web (see **Figure 6-29**).

Figure 6-29

Query1 : Select Query

candidate	Expr1001	Expr1002
▶ BUSH, GEORGE W	1358189	1820
BRADLEY, BILL	370238	602
GORE, AL	222491	354
MCCAIN, JOHN S	126040	263

In just a few steps, you have used all of SQL's basic commands, doing far less clicking and dragging than in the visual Query by Example method.

If you need to join tables, SQL also does that through one step — in the WHERE statement as we have previously mentioned.

Add the criminal and teacher tables in your query design and go to "SQL View" again. You will see that you have "SELECT FROM Criminals, Teachers" already in place. This time type "SELECT*" in the first line, and then type "WHERE criminals.lastname = teachers.lastname and criminals.firstname = teachers.firstname," as shown in **Figure 6-30.**

Figure 6-30

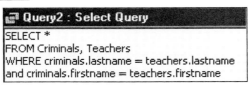

```
Query2 : Select Query
SELECT *
FROM Criminals, Teachers
WHERE criminals.lastname = teachers.lastname
and criminals.firstname = teachers.firstname
```

By running the query, you see how the tables were joined in **Figure 6-31.**

Figure 6-31

Criminals.Last	Criminals.First	Criminals.Date	Charge	Teachers.Last	Teachers.First	Teachers.Date
Barry	Donald	10/12/1955	Child molest	Barry	Donald	10/12/1955
Harwood	Mary	3/14/1969	Assault	Harwood	Mary	3/14/1969

SQL is well worth learning. It permits you to do queries faster, particularly those using Boolean logic. In addition, as you find yourself needing to clean or reshape data, SQL will go far beyond the point-and-click techniques by allowing you to trim out blank spaces, split fields into two and create programs that will rearrange data.

▼ CAR Wars

▼ The Dayton Daily News identified 30 cases of neglect by using a database of death cases and a database of group homes for the
▼ mentally retarded and documenting drowning of clients, the choking of clients, assaults and other forms of death.

▼   Overall the system of homes for the mentally retarded is cloaked in secrecy and difficult to obtain records from. To get around that,
▼ we matched the addresses of 400,000 death records with the addresses of dozens of group homes. Using the matches we found in the addresses, we then contacted family members and examined the inspection records of every group home.

We also talked to group home operators, advocates for the mentally retarded, surviving family members, caseworkers and state and local regulators. Our finding: Ohio's $1.85 billion system to protect 63,000 people with mental retardation is riddled with gaps that have deadly consequences.

As a result, the governor appointed a task force and the state auditor was asked to audit private companies under contract to provide care.

John Erickson, The Dayton Daily News

Chapter Checklist

- Database managers allow you to join two or more tables of information by matching names or identification numbers.

- You can join not only tables intended to be joined, but also those that no one had thought of joining to create enterprising stories.

- Structured Query Language (SQL) is part of most database managers and is a powerful program that can allow you to do many queries more simply and powerfully.

Your Turn to Practice

1 Get a relational database from the National Institute of Computer-Assisted Reporting called Tenncands. This database has two files: one of campaign donors and one of candidates.

2 Join the tables in the database.

3 Group and sum amounts by last name, then by occupation, then by contribution date. Sort each result by the highest amounts contributed.

4 Repeat the same query using candidates' names.

5 Do the same queries using Structured Query Language.

> ### www
> For more exercises in downloading and importing, go to
> **www.ire.org/carbook/chapter6**

PART **II**

Using Computer-Assisted Reporting in News Stories

CHAPTER 7

Getting Data
Not on the Internet

How to Find and Negotiate for Data

> *New Jersey state officials turned down the Asbury Park Press'*
> *request in the year 2000 for statistical reports that would help*
> *the paper measure the performance of the state's child protec-*
> *tion agency. But we learned of federal government databases*
> *that contained information on children in foster care through-*
> *out the United States, including New Jersey, and up to 1998.*
> *We also learned of a federal law that required the data to be*
> *released and used that knowledge to persuade the state offi-*
> *cials to release their data for 1999 and 2000.*
>
> *We succeeded in getting the electronic information necessary*
> *to examine the system and produce a five-day series that*
> *showed the state had done little to reform its system and that*
> *children were spending more time than ever in foster care and*
> *group homes.*
>
> — **Jason Method, Asbury Park Press**

Sometimes the database you need for a story is openly
distributed. Sometimes it is kept from you under the guise of
confidentiality or national security even though it would be easy
for officials to remove the sensitive material. Sometimes officials
try to withhold data by charging absurdly high prices for it.

What this means is that a journalist often may have to dig,
argue and push to get data that should be — and could be —
released almost immediately.

This chapter will look at the three steps — finding, negotiating and importing — for obtaining access to databases so that you can use them in a story. All three steps go together.

1. You need to *find* the right database for the story and the information you really need in it.
2. You often need to *negotiate* knowledgeably for the database and try to avoid stonewalling by bureaucrats who may snow you with technical terms. It is imperative that you acquire the supplementary material necessary to understand the database.
3. You need to know how to *import,* or transfer, the data from a diskette or other media source so that you can use it.

The basic principle to remember when seeking electronic information is that the keeper of public information must give you a good reason for *not* releasing that information. You, on the other hand, should not have to give the agency a good reason to release the information to you. Taxpayers have already supplied the money to enter the data, store the data and retrieve the data. In short, you need to think, but not necessarily say, "You have it. I want it. Give it to me."

Remember, a free and democratic society is based on openness, not bureaucracy and secrecy, and it is the journalist's duty and prerogative to pursue information.

▼ Finding Data

Often journalists who are just starting out in computer-assisted reporting wonder where they can find useful databases. The answer is "everywhere." We will focus on government databases because many private databases are not only hard to get but are priced well beyond the means of a journalist or newsrooms. In addition, many private and commercial databases are actually stitched together from public databases and with the skills learned in this book. Quite often, with basic skills you can do most of the linking of databases.

There are databases on almost any subject and at almost any agency. Since the proliferation of personal computers, most government agencies and businesses have been storing their information electronically. In addition, they have inventoried and indexed their databases more thoroughly, especially because of the so-called Y2K concerns prior to the year 2000, when agencies worried that their databases could be reduced to chaos because of date problems on January 1, 2000.

For example, the Federal Data Base Finder, which can be bought on CD-ROM for less than $60, lists thousands of federal databases. A sample listing from the CD-ROM is given in **Figure 7-1.**

Figure 7-1

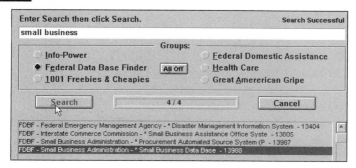

When you type "small business" in the search area, you can quickly search hundreds of database listings for any mention of small business. By moving the cursor down to the fourth listing at the bottom of the screen, clicking there and hitting "Enter," you can get the information shown in **Figure 7-2.**

Figure 7-2

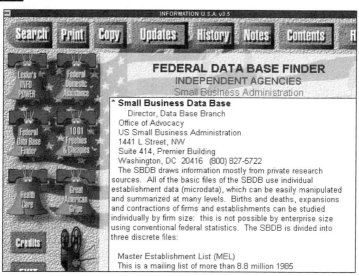

Each entry in the Federal Data Base Finder gives you a phone number and a description of a file. The Federal Data Base Finder also will lead you to unexpected places. For example, a search on the word *health* may turn up many entries from the Department of Agriculture. Over the past decade, there are more and more databases of databases. Individual states or vendors are listing databases, either in reports or online.

Even without these guides on a state level or local level, you know that most agencies are computerized and have extensive databases. When you walk into a state office, look around and you'll see everyone typing information into computers. At a city or town hall, you'll see the same thing whether you are at the building inspector's office or the recorder of deeds where real estate records are kept.

If you see a report with tables of columns and rows, there generally is a database behind the report, and you should get it if it looks useful for your work. State and federal housing agencies often issue reports about where subsidized housing is located, how many units are at that location and who can qualify for the housing. By asking for the backup electronic information on that report, a reporter can obtain not only the columns and rows that appear in the report, but also material that might have been excluded from the report such as politically embarrassing information.

It's also good to keep in mind that you may be seeing only a portion of a database when you see it on the Web. Often, databases on the Web are only summaries or portions of the original database. Often, the original database has information officials don't want released or don't realize could be of value to the public.

Although some states require agencies to provide lists of databases, many agencies may claim that a database doesn't exist because they don't want to be bothered with granting your request or because they have something to hide. But those same agencies may have hired consultants to unravel the mess the agencies made of their computer systems over the past two decades. The consultants issue reports, and in those reports are inventories of hardware, software and databases. The reports, particularly those done on the Y2K problems, can act as an index when you are trying to determine whether an agency has what you need. Ask the agency for copies of consultant reports on its computer systems.

Auditors' reports also generally contain an overview of an agency's records and how they are kept. The General Accounting Office, **www.gao.gov,** a congressional agency that does audits of federal agencies, actually uses many agencies' own databases to perform its audits. In the back of the GAO reports, the databases are described. Although the databases themselves may not be available online, reports, summaries and discussions of those databases are listed.

You can also look through commercial and governmental database catalogues. The catalogue put out by the commercial Dialog service lists databases you may have never considered. In some cases an agency staff member may be unaware of the agency's databases, but the database is listed at the federal National Technical Information Services (NTIS) or in its hard-copy catalogue.

In addition, developing source relationships with social scientists at universities and colleges can open up wide avenues of database possibilities. Those social researchers live in a world of databases because they rely on data for their statistical analyses.

If you cover a beat, you should develop sources at three levels or more. On the first level, talk to data-entry clerks who have few politics to play; they can tell you what kind of information they are entering. On the second level, talk to data processors; they can tell you what kind of information they are processing. On the third level, talk to administrators; they can tell you what kind of information they use for the reports they issue.

In some cases, administrators and their public information officers may not want to talk to the press or may even mislead reporters. That's why it's good to have sources at all three levels. Also, sometimes the administrators and information officers don't even know what a database is or what's in it.

There are also associations that you should know about or join. People who belong to groups that use SAS or SPSS (the statistical software packages) know about a wide range of data, from hospitals to insurance to government. The Association for Public Data Users (APDU) costs several hundred dollars a year to join, but if you can afford it, it's worth it. The APDU puts out a monthly newsletter that discusses public data.

▼ Obtaining Data

The first way to obtain a database is to ask for it. Do not write a formal request under the Freedom of Information Act or your state's or county's open records law. Just ask.

In a time of security-conscious officials, you may be required to put a request in writing, but this doesn't happen that often at the local level.

Some reporters carry blank diskettes so that they can ask for, and get, a copy of a small database before the bureaucratic shuffle and delay can begin. But if getting a database becomes cumbersome or the officials demand a formal request, then you will have to hunker down and do some planning.

To obtain a database, you need to know what to ask for. You need to know the laws and regulations governing the release of electronic information but not necessarily to use them as leverage. Sometimes you need to know them so you know you shouldn't bring them up. Some laws are so antiquated or ambiguous that officials can use the laws to effectively block the release of information. To get help on this, acquire the newly updated booklet or CD-ROM of "Access to Electronic Records," which summarizes the states' laws and gives advice on obtaining electronic information. The Reporters Committee for Freedom of the Press, **www.rcfp.org,** publishes and distributes the information and more.

Before you begin to battle for information, make sure you know what database you want and what part of it you need for the story. Conversely, know what you can give up. If you only need ZIP codes for your story, don't argue over street addresses.

Finally, you need to know how the information is stored. Is it on a personal computer? Is it on a mainframe? Is it in a spreadsheet, or database manager, or even in some ancient programming language? In what kind of format can the agency give it to you? What does the **record layout** look like? How many records are in the file and how large is the file? How many megabytes are in the file?

Answers to these questions will tell you what hardware, software and knowledge you need if you want to make good use of the data. If the information is on a personal computer, it will probably be easy to obtain in a usable form, but make sure you have at least three times the size of database available on your computer's hard drive. In order to process the data, you will need lots of space.

If the information is on a mainframe computer, you need to know whether the agency can copy the information onto CD-ROMs or only onto a computer tape. If it's on computer tape, you'll need to have access to another mainframe or a portable tape drive reader. Alternatively, you can ask the agency to put it on a Web site and allow you to download it.

The Record Layout

A record layout tells you the names of the columns, what types of data are in the column (text, numeric, date) and the width of each column. It's your road map to the structure of the database.

If the information is in a spreadsheet on a disk, chances are good that you won't need to know too much. With spreadsheets, you generally get the disk, copy information from the disk to your hard drive and open the file, and your own spreadsheet program puts the information on the spreadsheet grid. Like downloading data from the Internet, that's the easy way. Most of the time, however, you will get information that has been kept in a database manager, which you learned about in Chapters 5 and 6.

To understand the information in a database, you need a record layout. A record layout serves as a guide to how the information is stored and ordered and specifies the following.

- The name of each field.
- Whether it's a field that is text, also known as alphanumeric or character (consisting of letters and numbers), numeric (only numbers) or dates.
- How wide each field is. A field can contain only so many characters or numbers, depending on its width. (It's like filling out test forms that give you only 12 spaces for your last name. If your last name is Rumpelstiltskin, only "Rumpelstilts" will fit.)
- The position of the field in the record. If a record is 100 characters long and the last name field is the first field and 12 spaces wide, then the last name field's position is 1–12. Think of a record as a linear crossword puzzle.

Before acquiring a database, you should first get the record layout. The record layout will tell you what information is in the database and whether it fits your needs. You may need some explanation of the categories of information because sometimes they are abbreviated with acronyms. For example, you may find the category "CANDID," but this does not mean "candid"; it means "candidate identification number." **Figure 7-3** shows a modified record layout for individual contributors to federal political campaigns.

Figure 7-3

RECIPID	Character	9
AMENDMENT	Character	1
REPORT	Character	3
PRIMGEN	Character	1
MICROFILM	Character	11
CONTTYPE	Character	3
NAME	Character	50
CITY	Character	18
ZIP	Character	5
OCCUPATION	Character	35
CONTDATE	Date	8
AMOUNT	Numeric	7
OTHERID	Character	9
COMMCODE	Character	1
CANDID	Character	9

As you can see, the field names are somewhat cryptic. You can also see that the record length — if you add up all the fields — is 170 spaces. If you knew you were getting 10,000 records, you could calculate how big the file is. Multiply 170 times 10,000 and you get 1,700,000 bytes, or 1.7 megabytes — too big for a diskette. In addition, you will need the record layout if you are going to import the information into your own database manager software. By "import," we mean that you will transfer the information into your database while at the same time translating it into the programming language.

You also should obtain a **codebook** (or code sheet, which means the same thing) that goes with the data, if there is one. Why? Because to save space, a database maker does not want to write, for example, "black," "white" or "Hispanic." To save time on data entry and space, the database maker designs the ethnicity column to have only one character. The database maker codes blacks as "1," whites as "2" and

Hispanics as "3." You might be able to figure that out on your own, but you really don't want to get into a guessing game. So obtain the codebook or the code sheet. (Sometimes it is also called a data dictionary.)

You should also get a printout of the first 10 to 100 records to see if information has been entered into all the fields. You also need the printout to make sure that you have transferred the information properly into your computer. Also, get a hard copy of the form from which the information was entered. These are known as integrity checks, which will be covered in more detail in Chapter 9.

Computer Tapes

Government agencies and private businesses are continuing to replace 9-track computer tapes with smaller tapes, CD-ROMs and other forms of storage. The 9-track tape is the large reel of magnetic tape. (You might have seen them in the background of computer rooms in old science fiction movies.) The tapes, whether 9-track or newer tape cartridges, can be fragile and hard to deal with, but journalists will continue to encounter this obstacle for some time.

If the data are being delivered on a tape, you need to get the specifications.

- *The kind of language, or code, the information is in.* **EBCDIC** or **ASCII** is the choice. (EBCDIC stands for Extended Binary Coded Decimal Interchange Code. You pronounce it "ebb-see-dic." ASCII stands for American Standard Code for Information Interchange. You pronounce it "ask-key.") A personal computer reads ASCII; if the tape is in EBCDIC (which it will be if it comes from an IBM mainframe), you will have to translate it into ASCII. Don't worry — there are a lot of programs that do that. Many journalists use a software program called Nine-Track Express, which can be obtained from the National Institute for Computer-Assisted Reporting.
- *The kind of format.* If the data are not in a database or spreadsheet format, then generally you should ask for "fixed format," which means that all the information can be easily imported into a database manager. ASCII comma delimited is also acceptable. Most programs — whether they are spreadsheets or database managers — translate these formats.
- *The density of the tape.* Density means how many **bits** (remember that eight bits make up a **byte**) are squeezed onto eight of the nine tracks on the tape. The ninth track is used for checking the data.

• *The blocking factor.* To get more information on a tape, records are squeezed into blocks. If you have records that are 100 bytes long and you have a blocking factor of 10, it means that there are 1,000 bytes in each block. If the blocking factor is 20, then each block holds 2,000 bytes. This formula comes in handy when you want to make sure the agency gave you the right specifications. **Figure 7-4** shows what some tape specifications information looks like.

Figure 7-4

Density	6250 BPI (Bits per inch of tape)
Format	Fixed
Record length	100
Blocking factor	10
Block size	1000
Coding	EBCDIC
Number of records	851,777

To review, if you are given a diskette, you need to ask for (1) a record layout, (2) a code sheet, (3) a printout of the first 10 records and (4) what language the database is in.

If you are given a computer tape, you also need to ask the following questions.

• What language is it in — ASCII or EBCDIC?
• What is the format — fixed or other?
• What is the density — 6,250 **bpi** or other?
• What is the record length?
• What is the blocking factor?
• How many records will I receive?

This may seem way too technical or arcane, but you need to be aware of these specifications. Although you may get an academic or experts at NICAR to transfer the tape to CD-ROM and place it in a database for you, you still need to get these specifications for those that will help you.

▼ Privacy and Security Issues

Over the past decade, politicians and the public have become increasingly concerned about privacy and national security. They have denied requests for electronic information although it's available in hard copy or could be collated from public places. Jennifer LaFleur, a longtime practitioner and trainer in CAR, was once denied access to an Adopt-A-Highway electronic database. Officials said that under California law the information on names in the database was private even though the names are on public billboards where the donors claim credit for the upkeep of that portion of the highway.

In fact, a decade ago a group of journalists at a seminar compiled a list of 38 excuses bureaucrats gave for not releasing databases. (You can get the list from NICAR.) Some claimed it would take too much time or that they weren't sure how to make a copy of the data. The excuses on that list are still used today.

If an agency claims that its information is private or being withheld because of security reasons, you should check the laws and regulations. If the agency is right, you need to decide whether the rest of the information is still valuable.

Many reporters, by knowing what they need for a story, can agree to the deletion of certain categories. Sometimes you can give up the "name" field because you need the database for a demographic or statistical study. Reporters often give up names on medical or workers' compensation records because there are a large number of cases in open civil court that can be used for anecdotes.

If you are seeking state employee records, there are many stories you can do without getting street addresses. Rather than enter into year-long debates, you can give up some fields in exchange for the rest and still get your story.

▼ High Costs

News organizations have been asked to pay millions of dollars when their reporters are seeking information. Often the final cost has been a few hundred dollars or less. The state of Connecticut first asked The Hartford Courant for $3 million for drivers' license records. Three years later, after long negotiations, The Courant paid $1.

You can prevail on costs if you are willing to haggle and if you know what a fair price should be. Here are some guidelines.

- *The cost of the media.* A diskette or CD-ROM costs less than a dollar and a computer tape less than $20.
- *The cost of copying.* An agency should not charge you for copying information from the hard drive of a personal computer to a few disks. The cost of copying from a mainframe to a computer tape or disk should cost only a few dollars for what's known as runtime.
- *The cost of staff time.* Generally, the public has already paid for the collection and storage of data. Unless you ask for special programming, an agency should be hard-pressed to charge you for programming. If it does, the cost should not be more than $20 or $30 an hour. You should avoid programming whenever possible, because it means errors can be made and it gives the agency one more chance to take out records that might lead to an embarrassing story.

In practical terms, you should be able to obtain most databases for $100 or less. Even in those cases you should ask for a fee waiver because disclosure of this information is in the public's interest.

One threat to the open use of electronic records is the handling of public records by private vendors. Public agencies that don't have computer expertise often hire commercial vendors to do the work for them. But commercial vendors want to make a profit. If a citizen asks for the information, some commercial vendors will charge high costs for its copy of the files. Since some agencies don't have a copy of their own records, you then have to argue with the commercial vendor. Your best solution is to get your news organization and others to push for changing the law. In some states it is illegal for commercial vendors to charge exorbitant prices for public records.

▼ Importing

You don't want to go through all the work of obtaining a database and then not be able to use it. That's why you were careful to get the record layout, size of the file, code sheet and printout.

This book won't cover the importing of computer tapes, although many concepts used for importing from disks to hard drives are the same as the concepts for importing from computer tapes to hard drives.

There are two key points when you import data. One, make sure that the information goes into the correct columns and that those columns are labeled correctly. Two, make sure that the information is properly translated so that you can read it.

If you receive the data in one of the common database software programs, your job will be straightforward. Different databases previously tried not to translate the database software of other companies, but now they do. As an example, if you are importing a FoxPro file into Microsoft Access, you need only identify the kind of format the database is in and the information will automatically be loaded into Access. To get to the importing screen, you click on "Get External Data" under "File" on the Menu Bar and click on "Import," as shown in **Figure 7-5.**

Figure 7-5

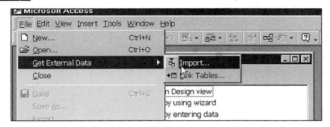

In **Figure 7-6,** you can import data in a common dBASE format or Excel or other formats. Note that there are many kinds of software Access can translate.

Figure 7-6

Sometimes you will receive information in ASCII, the common language of personal computers. ASCII files come in "fixed format" and "comma delimited," which are formats used for databases on the Web. Both kinds are shown in Chapter 2.

Comma delimited is used to save space. Instead of having blank spaces between columns, the columns are shoved together. Computer programs know to end a column when they see a comma. The quotation marks tell the software that the words in between should go into character fields. The other information is numeric. (In addition, you often can put field names in the first row to save yourself the time of typing them in again and again.)

Fixed format files are a little tricky because sometimes it is necessary to set up a file to catch the information in the proper column. But Access now has a Wizard just like Excel, and it will lead you through the same steps (see **Figure 7-7**).

Figure 7-7

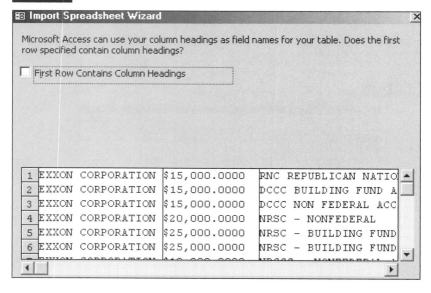

Finding and importing data can be tricky at times, but it's an integral part of computer-assisted reporting, and the more you do it, the easier it will become. Without the right data, you can't report accurately and completely on a story.

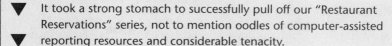

▼ CAR Wars

▼ It took a strong stomach to successfully pull off our "Restaurant Reservations" series, not to mention oodles of computer-assisted
▼ reporting resources and considerable tenacity.

▼ We began with several fundamental questions. We wondered whether area restaurants were generally following or failing the rules; whether the government's system of overseeing restaurants
▼ was working; and whether the average consumer had any way to distinguish between the safe and unsafe.

Some government agencies resisted our request for inspection data and only relented after official requests, meetings and follow-up phone calls and e-mails. Even then, some took weeks or months to provide records. The state Department of Health failed to provide complete data for six months, and only after we noticed that the computer file they initially provided was incomplete.

Be careful what you ask for, because you just might get it. That's how we felt after the various agencies' data arrived. There were different formats, missing records, duplicate records and data from ancient computer systems.

But in total we found area restaurants had violated food-safety rules more than 130,000 times over a five-year period, with 20,000 of those as critical. As for enforcement, we found penalties against violators were rare, even when they were proven to have made people sick.

Rick Linsk, The St. Paul Pioneer-Press

 Chapter Checklist

- You can locate databases by looking for computers on your beat or asking where printouts come from.

- Federal and state agencies are putting more and more of their database listings online, yet at the same time closing off certain information because of security and privacy concerns.

- Consultants and auditors identify databases in their reports that you might not know about otherwise.

- Always get proper documentation for a database, and always try to get the database for free.

- Know the laws relating to electronic access.

- Most database manager and spreadsheet software can import most files.

Your Turn to Practice

1 Prepare to request electronic information from the local city or county for names, titles, departments and salaries for all employees. Make a checklist of what you need.

2 Go to the Reporters Committee on Freedom of the Press Web site, **www.rcfp.org,** and see the resources available there.

3 Read your state's open records law. Make notes.

4 Check your state's attorney general Web site for any opinions relating to your request.

5 Request the record layout of a database of salary information and code sheets.

6 Request to see a printout of some of the records.

7 Be prepared to write an open records request so you are ready if they ask for a written request.

8 Import the data into a database manager.

9 Analyze and find out who gets paid the most and what the average and median wages are.

> ### www
> For more exercises in downloading and importing, go to
> **www.ire.org/carbook/chapter7**

CHAPTER **8**

Building Your Own Database

How to Develop Exclusive Sources

> We wanted to examine how Swedish authorities attacked
> financial crime in their country. We built our own database of
> complaints and suspects from three agencies and by looking
> through several hundred records built the profile of the average
> suspect and complaint. We determined that the authorities
> were not pursuing big-time crooks, but instead were sitting
> back and dedicating their time to prosecuting small business
> owners with bookkeeping trouble.
>
> — **Swedish broadcasters Helena Bengtsson and Jenny Nordberg**

By building their own database, Bengtsson and Nordberg
joined hundreds of other reporters both in the United States
and throughout the world over the past decade in learning to
effectively create databases for better journalism. Knowing how
to build a database is a skill that helps journalists practicing
computer-assisted reporting because it means they don't have to
rely only on databases created by others.

Journalists outside the United States have significantly less
access to data in their countries and often find they need to get
paper records and then enter information from those records
into a spreadsheet or database manager. But U.S. journalists —
especially in small towns or on campuses — have to create databases much more often than was supposed.

There are many times when the information you want —
especially on the local level — is not in electronic form. Furthermore, despite open records laws, recalcitrant officials refuse to

obey those laws, as discussed in Chapter 7. Those officials needlessly delay their responses to requests, set high prices or cite privacy and security issues to deny access to public data. Consequently, when you can't obtain data in a timely manner, you might have to take up the challenge of building your own databases. Sometimes the creation of your own database is quick and easy. Sometimes data entry and checks on the accuracy of data entry can be time-consuming. To build any database requires some forethought, efficient scheduling and an enterprising spirit.

But the payoff is well worth it. You know intimately how accurate the information is. It is the database you really need for the story, and not one that will have to be worked with extensively to find what you need. You also can enter the information you want in the format you want it. And it provides you with exclusive and frequently powerful stories on which you can report with authority, citing patterns and trends that otherwise would have gone unnoticed.

Last, the knowledge of how to build a database makes you more valuable in your news organization and more competitive with other news organizations. Clearly, this is a skill worth having.

Over the past decade numerous journalists have built their databases on a wide range of international, national and local issues. They include databases on deaths from the terrorist attacks on the World Trade Center, fatalities at racecar events, the resale of badly damaged salvage vehicles, employee attendance problems at county agencies and court-houses, questionable pawnshop transactions, immigrant workers' abuse, sentencing of criminals, lobbyists' gifts to legislators and backgrounds of riverboat pilots.

Some journalists also build databases to keep track of contacts and sources. Jo Craven McGinty, an expert in computer-assisted reporting and a Pulitzer Prize winner, not only did extensive data analysis on police shootings while at The Washington Post, but also kept a database log of contacts with other metropolitan police departments across the United States. When those department officials claimed to forget she had requested information, she could — by referring to her database — cite the date and time of her last call and the person she had talked to. In many cases, the police officials became much more cooperative when confronted with that information.

While at The Hartford Courant, I built databases on environmental pollution, lobbyists, campaign finance and early retirement pensions. But a database I and two other reporters created on murders possibly in-volving a serial killer resulted in stories with one of the greatest impacts.

Hearing that police were looking at potential links among murders of women in the Hartford area, I decided to look at newspaper clippings of unsolved murders of women in Connecticut during the past five years. There were about 40 such cases, and we decided to enter demographic information about the victims in a database manager to see if there were any apparent connections. We included the name of each victim, how she was killed, where she was from and when she was found. Not all of the information was available. Still, we had enough to work with, and we started to filter the information by selecting the town the victim was from.

The town in which a body is found dictates which police department investigates. This means that if a killer disposes of his victims in different towns, then police may be slower to see the links than if the killer is disposing of victims in just one town. The local police and medical examiner's office had been investigating the homicides by the town in which each victim was *found*. By looking at the town the victim was *from*, we clearly saw patterns.

First, I ran a query to view those from Hartford. By looking at the detailed information on these individuals, I found that five of the women had last been seen in the same neighborhood in Hartford. **Figure 8-1** shows part of the actual database. (With the reporters, we were able to fill in some of the missing information through interviews and by obtaining a medical examiner's database and using the FBI supplementary homicide database.)

Figure 8-1

Lastname	Firstname	Middleinitial	Street	Town	State	Found
MAYO	TAMEIKA			HARTFORD	CT	ROCKY HILL
TERRY	CARLA			HARTFORD	CT	WINDSOR
RIVERA	SANDRA			HARTFORD	CT	SOUTH WINDSOR
DANCY	DIEDRE			HARTFORD	CT	HARTFORD
PEREZ	EVELYN			HARTFORD	CT	WETHERSFIELD
PEEBLES	PATRICIA			HARTFORD	CT	NEWINGTON
PARRENO	MARIA			HARTFORD	CT	HARTFORD

We looked at further details of the crimes, interviewed family members and gathered more information from a medical examiner's database. We also found two other clusters of murders. Law enforcement officials then formed a task force to study the possible connections to all the killings, which until then had not been linked.

Within a year, some law enforcement officials were convinced that not one but three serial killers were operating in the state. Officials arrested one suspect and stepped up their investigations. More important, the Hartford killings stopped.

Other reporters have also created databases for their stories. As mentioned in Chapter 2, Mike Berens, then at The Columbus Dispatch in Ohio, created his own database and used similar techniques to track an interstate serial killer around the same time; and reporters at the Seattle Times also created a database on serial killings. In each of these cases, the database provided tips, illustrated possible patterns and provided a significant stepping-off point for the journalists.

▼ When to Build

Anthony DeBarros, who helped create a database on victims of the terrorist attacks at the World Trade Center, said that USA Today decided to go forward because the reporters knew at a minimum that a verified list of victims' identities would help with follow-up stories and could provide the basis for enterprise work.

Indeed, the newspaper broke stories that showed in scrupulous detail how the location of a person's office and the building design affected his or her chance of survival. The database also provided leads to survivors and other stories on rescue efforts and many other stories. It also allowed the newspaper to deal with the confusion about victims that plagued government agencies. "Confronted with such a complex web of facts . . . a database is truly the best tool for unearthing trends that make for compelling stories," DeBarros said.

Deciding to build a database should be based on a group of factors.

- Certainty that the information does not exist in some kind of electronic form already
- A minimum purpose or a minimum story for which the database can be used, whether it is to keep track of complex information over time or to provide the context for at least one important story
- Whether the database will be a useful archive and whether reporters can add to it for future stories
- How many categories (columns or fields of information) will be required and how many records will have to be entered
- A realistic schedule on the time to create the database
- Having the staff required to create the database

Once you consider those factors, you can make a well-informed decision about whether to begin.

▼ Spreadsheet or Database Manager

For smaller amounts of information, a spreadsheet is a good tool with which to build a database. A spreadsheet doesn't require first creating a structure in which to enter the data. What you see is what you get. (You can type the information into a worksheet from the examples of smaller datasets shown in Chapter 3.)

This means it is easy to label the columns (or categories) of information, type in the information and analyze it right away. But if there are many categories of information (more than 20 or 30) and many records (more than a few hundred) to be entered, it's worth taking the time to consider working in a database manager.

A database manager is designed to deal with more complex information. It can also streamline data entry by allowing you to use a relational database that enables you to enter basic information once rather than many times. As we saw in Chapter 6, data entry of political contributions into two tables meant that the candidates' information did not have to be entered more than one time.

Placing data in a database manager also means you have the option of linking your database to other databases created by government agencies or businesses. Whether you choose a spreadsheet or database manager, the good news is that once information is in an electronic column and row format it can be easily imported into other software.

▼ Using the Database Manager

Since it's pretty self-evident on how to put data into a spreadsheet, we will focus on creating a database in a database manager. Many reporters initially build a database to keep track of information about political contributors. A political database might include the contributor's name, street, city, state, amount given, to whom it was contributed and the date of contribution.

In a database manager, you need to set up a structure within which to keep the information. This is the same tool known as a *record layout* discussed in Chapter 7. If the information contains both words and numbers, you want the type to be in "character" or "text" or "alphanumeric" form.

If it contains numbers that you might want to add, subtract, divide or multiply, the type should be numeric. If the information is a date, you want to use the date type. This allows you to calculate the number of days between dates, group by dates and sort by dates. For example, you might want to see on which dates traffic accidents most often occurred. Or you might want to calculate the actual time served in prison by felons.

Unlike a spreadsheet, where you can type without regard to column width, in a database you need to think about how many spaces or characters a field will take (just like a crossword puzzle). Most last names can be contained in 25 characters. States are always two characters. ZIP codes are five or nine characters long. If you choose numeric, a database manager generally will make sure you have enough room.

Let's look at how you would set up a structure in a database manager. In Microsoft Access, you would open a new database as in **Figure 8-2.**

Figure 8-2

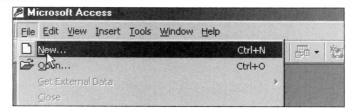

Then click on "Database," as in **Figure 8-3.**

Figure 8-3

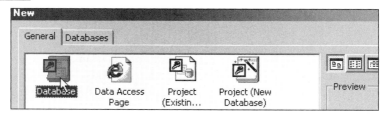

When you click on "Database," you will be asked to name the database in which you will build your tables, as shown in **Figure 8-4.** We will call this database "campaign finance" and place it in a folder called "politics." (Remember that a database itself in Access is like a subfolder in which files are placed.)

Figure 8-4

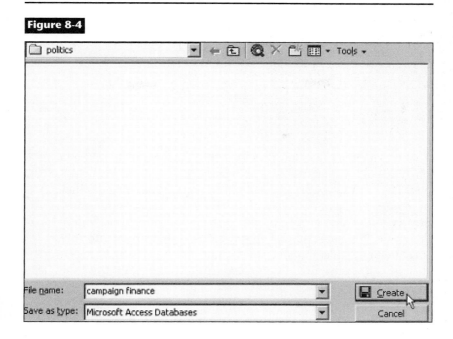

Now click on "Create," and you will be taken to your database, where you can create tables using Design view, as shown in **Figure 8-5.**

Figure 8-5

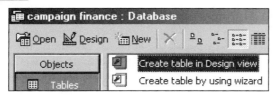

When you double-click on "Create table in Design view," you are taken to a grid where you can start to build your own table, as shown in **Figure 8-6.**

Figure 8-6

Table1 : Table		
Field Name	Data Type	Description
▶		

As in Chapter 7, you must be concerned with key areas of the table: the name of the field, the type of data and the width of the field. Let's create our first table on candidates' information that includes their ID number, name, party, street address, city, ZIP code, election year and district. (Normally, we would split up the name into at least four fields — last name, first name, middle initial, suffix — and streets into at least three fields — street number, street name and street suffix. This ensures that we can sort by any of those fields later. However, for this example, we will take a shortcut — just like many government agencies do.)

Let's name the first field "ID" and choose "Text" as in **Figure 8-7.**

Figure 8-7

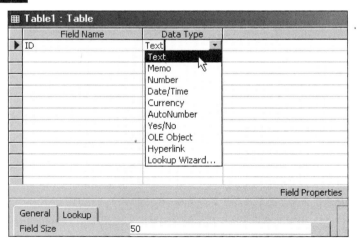

Note that you have many choices of "Data Type." In this chapter, we will use the three major types: "Text," "Number" and "Date/Time." Also, note that, in the lower window, "Field Size" (the number of letters or numbers that fit in the field) is automatically 50. We will change this to

9, since that is the exact amount of numbers that are used in a federal candidate's ID number, as shown in **Figure 8-8.**

Figure 8-8

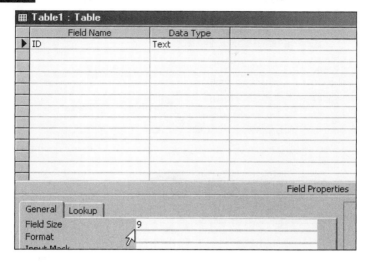

Next, type in "Candidate" for the name, choose "Text" and leave the "Field Size" at 50, as shown in **Figure 8-9.**

Figure 8-9

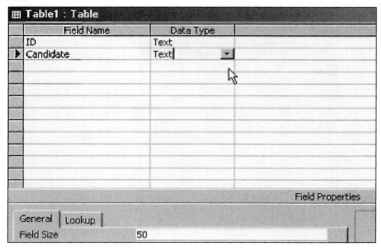

Continue putting in field names and deciding on the field size as you go. When you get to "State" as in **Figure 8-10,** for example, change the size to 2, since state (post office) abbreviations are only two letters.

Figure 8-10

On the next field, "Zip," you can choose 5 or 10, since ZIP codes in the United States can be either 5 digits or 9 digits with a hyphen. You keep "Zip" as a text field, as in **Figure 8-11,** because you will never add or subtract the numbers. Also, if you make "Zip" numeric and the code starts with "0," the program may eliminate it and you will have a meaningless 4-digit ZIP code (see **Figure 8-11**).

Figure 8-11

You can now finish the table by typing in election "Year" and "District." Election "Year" is two spaces and "District's" field size is two spaces. Go to "File" on the Menu Bar and click on "Save As." Then name the new table "CANDS," as in "candidates" as shown in **Figure 8-12.**

Figure 8-12

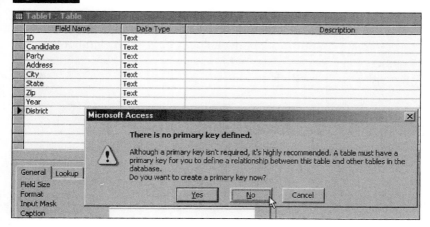

When you click on "OK," the program will ask if you want to create a "primary key." That means it will automatically give each record a number that you might use to link with other tables. In this case, each candidate will already have an "ID" number, so you click on "No" as in **Figure 8-13.**

Figure 8-13

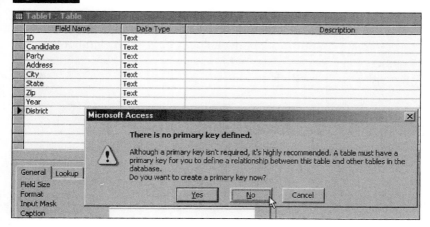

When you click on "No," you are returned to the original screen that you started from, and there is your table "CANDS," as shown in **Figure 8-14.**

Figure 8-14

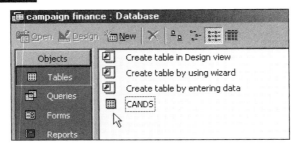

Click on the box next to "CANDS" and you go to a screen where you begin typing in data just as you do in a spreadsheet. You can fill the fields in each record in any order you want, as in **Figure 8-15,** and enter entire records in any order you want, since a database manager makes data so flexible and easy to sort.

Figure 8-15

	ID	Candidate	Party
▶		BUSH, GEORGE W	REP
*			

As you see, with a little modification and changes in field names, you can create your own electronic Rolodex or keep any kind of list of names. You could add dates of birth, ages or other demographic information such as ethnicity.

▼ Creating a Relational Database

A single table is sometimes called a "flat file" because it doesn't connect with other tables. In the example of campaign finance, we know that we now want to add another table and link it to the candidates' names through the candidates' ID numbers.

Once again, we click on "Create table in Design view." When we come to the grid, we want to type in the Field Names "Lastname," "Restofname," "City," "State," "Zip," "Occupation," "Cont_date" (for contribution date), "Amount" and "Cand_ID." We use the underscores so that the program sees the field name as one word. Sometimes database managers, particularly when you are using SQL, have problems with spaces. The Cand_ID, as in Chapter 6, is the key field linking the "CANDS" table to the new table, which we will call "GIVE." **Figure 8-16** shows what the GIVE table looks like when completed.

Figure 8-16

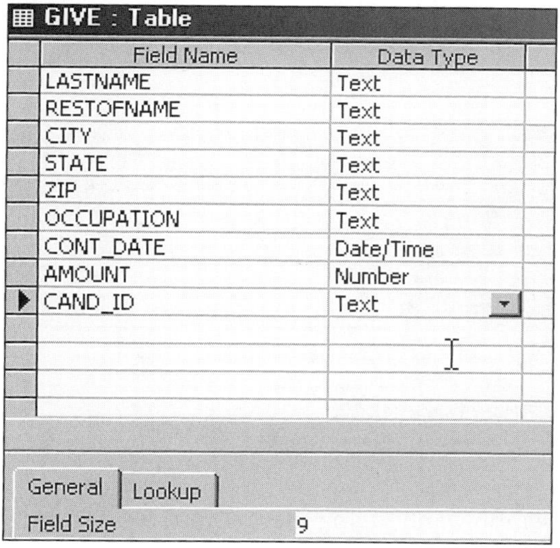

GIVE : Table

Field Name	Data Type
LASTNAME	Text
RESTOFNAME	Text
CITY	Text
STATE	Text
ZIP	Text
OCCUPATION	Text
CONT_DATE	Date/Time
AMOUNT	Number
► CAND_ID	Text

General | Lookup
Field Size   9

Note that under "Data Type," we put "Date/Time" next to "Cont_date" because that field will contain the date the contribution was made. By having the "Data Type" in the "Date" format, we can calculate the differences in dates or determine ranges of dates.

Note, we chose "Number" for "Data Type" for the field "Amount" because we plan to do math — addition and subtraction — with the numbers in that field. We also can limit the amount that can be typed in through the use of the "Validation Rule" line. This line says data entered outside the limits are not valid.

Most campaign finance laws limit the amount of contributions an individual can make to a single candidate. Let's say in this example you can't give more than $2,000. By typing "<2001" in the "Validation Rule" line, we can make sure we don't type a number higher than that when doing data entry. (If there is a higher number on a hard-copy report from which you are typing, then you have found an error in how someone recorded the contribution — or a very interesting story.) In addition, you can type a message in the "Validation Text" line that will show up if you make a mistake. **Figure 8-17** shows these additions to the table.

Figure 8-17

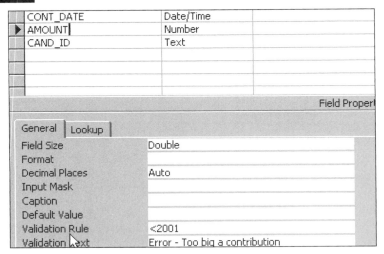

After closing the window and saving the changes, we can try typing 3000 — for $3,000 — into the "Amount" field. When we try to enter the data, we get the message shown in **Figure 8-18.**

Figure 8-18

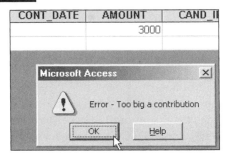

Now that you have created two tables, you can begin the data entry. By keeping the candidates' ID numbers consistent, you have established a relational database. If you create a new query in your database, you can add the two tables to your query screen and link them through ID number (see **Figure 8-19**), just as we did in Chapter 6.

Figure 8-19

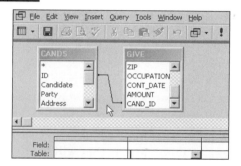

These are the basic steps in creating your own database. With a little practice, you will see constant opportunities to create small or large databases for stories. These databases will lead to tips and much better documented stories or just better recordkeeping.

▼ CAR Wars

▼ River pilots have one of the most dangerous jobs in Louisiana, but we didn't think the issue was that provocative when we first
▼ decided to take a look at the people who guide foreign-flagged vessels along the Mississippi River.
▼   At the time, we wanted to find out if two rumors were true: that Louisiana pilots are some the highest paid mariners in the country
▼ and that widespread nepotism makes it virtually impossible for nonrelatives to join the ranks.

The main records we wanted were their job applications and the accident reports they filled out. We wound up with six boxes of documents and it took three weeks to type everything we needed into Excel spreadsheets.

The results were irrefutable: Of the 100 people selected to become river pilots in recent years, 85 were related to other pilots.

> We further analyzed our database with both Excel and Access and found serious problems with overall pilot discipline involving lack of punishment and drug abuse.
>
> **Jeffrey Meitrodt,** The Times-Picayune

 ## Chapter Checklist

- Database managers allow you to build your own tables of information.

- Building your own tables can ensure that the data is accurate and will serve the needs of your story.

- You must plan ahead when building your database so that you know that it will have a minimum purpose that will justify the time spent constructing it.

- If you build a good database, it will organize your recordkeeping, provide tips for stories and help you see trends and patterns.

- When building a table, always think of possible key fields that will allow you to link the table to other tables.

 ## Your Turn to Practice

1 Using Excel, build a database of your family and friends with each's last name, first name, middle initial, street number, street name, street suffix, city, state, ZIP code, phone number, e-mail, date of birth, sex and age. Enter at least 10 records.

2 Find the average age and median age in your table of family and friends.

3 Using Access, build a table of your family and friends. Enter at least 10 records.

4 Find the average age in your table. (*Hint:* You can find the average when you use the "Totals" line in your queries.)

www
For more exercises in building a database, go to **www.ire.org/carbook/chapter8**

CHAPTER 9
Dirty Data

How to Fact-Check Your Data and Clean It

> *When the statewide information on Florida designer-drug deaths arrived, it quickly became obvious that the study was riddled with mistakes. In case after case, the victims appeared too young or too old to be designer-drug users. And records showed that it was unlikely that many of the cases had been scrutinized before. Those cases included terminal cancer patients who shot themselves, nursing home patients who fell and a four-year-old boy treated for spinal meningitis.*
> — **Hanque Curtis, The Orlando Sentinel**

Once you start using these computer-assisted reporting techniques, it won't be long before you both hear and ask this question: "How dirty is the data?" (Even most computer nerds don't say, "How dirty *are* the data?")

Dirty data usually begin with sloppy typing. Remember that someone who was doing one of the most boring jobs in the world has entered the information into a database. Agencies and businesses pay low wages to data-entry clerks, which increases low morale. Often, an agency is too understaffed to do proper data-integrity checks. If the agency does do integrity checks, there is still the possibility of erroneous information not being corrected.

Whenever you obtain a new database, always browse through the top 100 records to look for misspellings and nonsense. You also should run queries in a database manager that use the distinct function and the "Group By" statement to see patterns of bad data entry. For example, if the database contains town names, run a query that asks how many distinct spellings there are. (Often the same town is spelled several different ways.) If the database (e.g., about truck accidents) contains designations for interstate highways, "Interstate 70" might appear as I-70, Interstate 70 and I 70. Other federal or state records might spell "St. Louis" as Saint Louis, St. Louis and St Louis.

This hurts your ability to do accurate analyses unless you clean the data or do manual calculations. Remember that to a computer a space and a hyphen make the information look different. To a database manager, St. Louis and St Louis are different towns.

The lesson is that you must never implicitly trust the data. No database is perfect, and no database is complete. Every database is likely to contain a misleading or tricky field. Indeed, George Landau, a computer-assisted reporting expert, says that all databases are bad databases. You just have to find out how bad it is, what its flaws are, and if it has enough accurate data to be helpful.

Good journalists have always known that they shouldn't trust what anyone tells them until they check the information. (The cliché is that if your mother tells you she loves you, you should check it out.) That same skepticism must be applied to databases. The world is not a perfect place. People are not perfect. If we are working on a story, we try to determine how much one person really knows and then interview another two or three people to cross-reference and verify what they told us. We should apply these same methods to databases.

Before you begin the traditional reporting, you must immediately run these data checks and decide if you need to clean the data and how much of it to clean. Without doing this first, you will be misled just as though a source gave you the wrong tip.

A good example has been the trap in a U.S. government contract database in the years prior to 2001 that has almost snagged many a journalist. The database contains items such as the agency that awarded the contract, the company that received it, the amount, the year and the place where work on the contract will be carried out. Lurking in the database is a field of information called "type of obligation." The field contains one character of information — either "A" or "B" — right after the "dollars" field. Part of the actual layout is shown in **Figure 9-1**.

Figure 9-1

Data Element	Data	Chars.	Position
Dollars (in thousands)	N	8	315-322
Type of Obligation	A	1	323

If you don't pay attention to the "type of obligation" field, you can end up with completely erroneous data. Why? Because all the dollar amounts posted in the contract database are positive. If the obligation type is "A," the dollar amount remains positive. If the obligation type is "B," however, that tells you the contract was de-obligated — that is, withdrawn — and the dollar amount should be read as negative. It also means that you must multiply any dollar amount by –1 if the obligation type is "B."

There is no problem if you know to ask what "obligation type" means or if the agency that distributes the data tells you its meaning, but that is not always the case. In fact, several journalists have narrowly dodged the statistical bullet only because they thought to recheck the database, compare it with paper summary reports and check back with the agency. If they had neglected to multiply certain dollar amounts by –1, they would have been off by hundreds of millions of dollars when they added up the dollar column.

▼ Kinds of Pitfalls

Dirty databases and shoddy documentation come in many forms, including the following.

- Inaccurate record layouts, code sheets and record counts
- Typos or a lack of standardization in the spelling of names and places in the database
- Incomplete data entry
- Programming characters such as icons or blanks in the data
- Data with headers because it was copied from a file that was meant to be a printout
- Inaccurate importing or downloads by the agency or the journalist

These problems are more common than they should be, but they can be identified and often corrected.

▼ Two Rules

Before we look at these problems — and the solutions — there are two cardinal rules in dealing with dirty data. First, never work on the original database. Create a copy of the database and do your work there. If you make a mistake, you want to be able to recover and start again. You can't do that if you changed the original file. Also, as you work with the data, save each major change to the data as a different file, with sequential numbering. This creates an audit trail of your work. For example, working with census data, your first census file might be "states1." The copy would be "states2," the next copy "states3." Second, if you need to standardize spellings, never do it in the original field. Always create a new field next to it. That way you don't change the original, which can act as a reference point with which you can check your cleaning.

▼ Record Layout

First, we need to review a record layout. From the previous chapter, you know why you need a record layout if you are going to acquire a database. As we have said, the record layout acts as a road map to the database. It tells you the name of the field of information; whether the field contains letters and numbers, just numbers or dates; and the width of the column, which indicates how many letters or numbers can fit in the particular column.

You also know from the previous chapter that you need the code sheet or codebook that goes with the database. Without the codes, you cannot know that "1" means white or that "4" means felony.

You also know you may have to argue and plead to obtain a database, possibly spending months persuading a bureaucrat to give it to you. And you know that once you have it, you will be pleased that you won the battle. Unfortunately, you may find that obtaining the database is only the beginning of the struggle.

▼ Record Layout Miscues

Many journalists doing computer-assisted reporting have discovered errors in the record layout, the codebook and the information itself.

Moreover, the record layout does not promise that every field has data in it.

For example, FBI crime statistics for several states do not list rapes because of a disagreement over the definition of "rape." Moreover, state bail databases often lack the critical information about whether a defendant *could* post bond and get out of jail. Sometimes the agency has removed, or redacted, the information without saying so. Let's look at some of the possible problems in record layouts.

The sample layout in **Figure 9-2** shows how the information might appear within the columns.

Figure 9-2

Field	Type	Length
First name	Character	15
Last name	Character	20
Agency	Character	20
Salary	Numeric	6

In this example, you look at the information before importing it into your database manager. You see the first two records, which are shown in **Figure 9-3.**

Figure 9-3

Paula	Jones	Social Services	15541	10/12/1991
Dawn	Brown	Comptroller	21203	05/06/1989

Already you notice that something looks wrong. According to **Figure 9-2,** there should be only four columns of information. But in **Figure 9-3,** there is an extra column of information that looks like a date. What probably happened is that when the database was first put together, the database designer decided not to include the date of hire. Later, the designer thought the date of hire should be included.

When you are ready to import information into your database manager, you may have to set up the structure to hold the information. The database structure generally is a mirror of the record layout, as you saw in the last chapter. In this example, the database structure you set up (shown in **Figure 9-4**) would look like the record layout given in **Figure 9-2.**

Figure 9-4

Field Name	Data Type	
Firstname	Text	Should be 15 in width
Lastname	Text	Should be 20 in width
Agency	Text	Should be 20 in width
Salary	Number	Defaults to correct width

Table1 : Table

But if you imported the information shown in **Figure 9-3** into that layout, it would fall into the wrong fields. The first few records might look like those shown in **Figure 9-5.**

Figure 9-5

Firstname	Lastname	Agency	Salary
Paul	Jones	Social Services	15541
10/20/91	Dawn	Brown	Comptroller

As you can see, the information has shifted and is now falling into the wrong fields.

A real-life instance of the problem of shifting information happened not to a journalist but to the federal court system in Connecticut. In Hartford, the court system used a voter list to send out notices for jury duty. To get people's names, the court imported a voter registration list into a database it created. Well, Hartford has a large minority population, whereas towns outside Hartford are largely white. Lawyers soon started to notice that the prospective jurors for federal court were mostly white. Eventually, an investigation found that data processors for the court had misread the record layout for voter registration. Instead of allowing eight spaces for the town's name, Hartford, they allowed only seven spaces. Thus, "Hartford" was chopped off at "Hartfor." The truncation would not have been a problem except that the following field gave the person's life status. Because the record layout was wrong, the "d" just moved into the next field. In that field, "d" stood for "dead." Of course, the court didn't want to send jury summonses to dead people, so it had created a program that did not include anyone with a status of "d" on its mailing list. To the court's computer, everyone in Hartford was dead. Since no one from Hartford received a jury summons, there were few people of color on the juries. Clearly, it is important to check the record layout against the actual data. It is not uncommon to be given an old record layout or an incomplete one.

▼ Cryptic Codes

Probably more common than a bad record layout is an incomplete or inaccurate code sheet. In the previous chapter, you learned why you need the code sheet or codebook. The codes must be translated, or you'll be lost in a forest of numbers. But first you need to make sure the codes are accurate.

Let's say you obtain a code sheet that defines ethnicity by numbers: "1" for white, "2" for black, "3" for Hispanic and "4" for other. Once you have imported the information into your database, you perform a standard integrity check. You run a query that asks for the number of records for each race. **Figure 9-6** shows the query, which is the powerful "Group By" query you learned in Chapter 5.

Figure 9-6

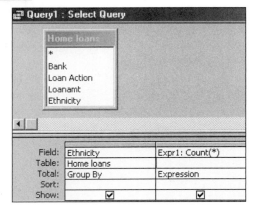

The result is shown in **Figure 9-7.**

Figure 9-7

Ethnicity	Totals
1	550
2	430
3	255
4	77
7	2
8	1
9	113

What's going on? Why are there so few totals for ethnic groups 7 and 8? Well, the "7" or "8" could be data-entry errors. No one can type hundreds or thousands of numbers without getting a few wrong. After calling the agency, you can probably throw those out. But the "9" cannot be ignored. You call the agency again and learn that they have decided to use "9" when the information wasn't submitted. But they forgot to put that on their code sheet.

In another example, you might be given all the expenditures for every agency in a state. The agencies are listed not by name but by identification numbers, which range from 1001 through 4999. You run a query in which you group the identification numbers and sum the amount column. **Figure 9-8** shows what the top of the result might look like.

Figure 9-8

Agency	Total (in thousands)
1022	255,321
4077	121,444
5019	23,655

The result includes an agency identification number, 5019, that does not exist on the code sheet. This actually happens quite frequently. For example, many states add and eliminate agencies after the election of a new governor. Often, new identification numbers are added to the database but not to the code sheet. If they are added to a code sheet, they may only be a collection of scribbles on the database administrator's copy.

▼ Sorry, Wrong Number

The opening discussion of this chapter indicated that it's easy to make mistakes in the millions. You must check to see that all the numbers add up, or at least come close. In the previous chapter you learned to (1) ask how many records you would receive in a database and (2) ask for hard-copy reports.

You also need to do an outer integrity check, which means comparing your analysis to something outside the database such as a written summary report by the agency or an auditor. In fact, journalists performed an outer check to find out about obligation type in the anecdote about the federal contracts database. The outer check in that case involved finding a hard-copy report that totaled the amount of federal contracts for each state and compared it to the totals from the database. For federal contracts, you would group the agencies and sum the dollars. Then you would compare the sum for each agency with a hard-copy report.

An outer integrity check not only protects against errors, but can lead to excellent news stories. Elliot Jaspin, a pioneer in computer-assisted reporting, performed a simple integrity check when he received a computer tape of low-interest mortgages given out by a state agency to low- and moderate-income people in Rhode Island. Working at The Providence Journal Bulletin at the time, Jaspin totaled the amount of mortgages in the database and compared his figure to the totals published in an annual report. The difference was millions of dollars.

But Jaspin had not made a mistake. Apparently, the agency had been hiding a slush fund out of which it made loans to the unqualified friends and relatives of politicians. A phone call from Jaspin about the discrepancy worried the agency, which began shredding documents. Soon thereafter the state police raided the agency, and investigations ensued.

Dollar amounts are not the only thing that can go awry. One quick outer integrity check can involve counting the number of records in your database and comparing it with the number the agency said it gave you. If the numbers don't match, you have a serious problem.

However, the situation can be worse. When it is worse, you need to think of all the integrity checks you can do. I once asked for attendance records for 10,000 state employees. The records showed how the employees spent every working hour — whether it was regular time, overtime, sick time, vacation or personal days. The agency that gave me the records said it had forgotten to do a record count, but because it gave me 1.8 million attendance records, which is what I had counted, I thought I had them all.

However, after a while it occurred to me that I probably should have records for at least 250 days for each employee. Even if an employee left partway through the year, another employee would be earning overtime. A quick calculation of 10,000 employees times 250 days results in 2.5 million records. It took two days of debate, but the agency finally looked at its own work, found a serious programming error and acknowledged that it had shorted me 700,000 records.

▼ Where Is the Standard?

One of the most onerous database problems is the lack of standardization. Names can be spelled several different ways or different words used for the same category, such as "attorney" or "lawyer." It can be time-consuming to fix these problems, but sometimes it's the only way if you want to get accurate counts and summaries.

Let's say you have a database of gun dealers, and you want to count the number in St. Louis. The field name in the government database is "PREMCITY," as in where the premises are of the story. If you run a query to count them, you will get a display as shown in **Figure 9-9.**

Figure 9-9

PREMCITY	COUNT
St Louis	22
St. Louis	24
Saint Louis	4

With a pencil or calculator, you could add this up to 50, but if you have a lot of records, you wouldn't want to do that. You might use a "where" statement, with a wildcard, that looks at the string of letters, but a better approach involves adding a field called "NEWPREMCITY." In Access, you can create a new field by using "Insert" in the Menu Bar, as in **Figure 9-10.**

Figure 9-10

After clicking on "Insert" and "Rows," you will have a new line in which you can enter "NEWPREMCITY," as in **Figure 9-11.**

Figure 9-11

Field Name	Data Type
PREMCITY	Text
NEWPREMCITY	Text
PREMST	Text
PREMZIP	Text
MAILADD	Text
MAILCITY	Text
MAILST	Text

Once you have a new field, you can use an "Update" statement in a "Query" to define all possible spellings of the name. This tells the database manager to change the names to one spelling and put the changes in "NEWPREMCITY." To use the "Update," go through the process of getting to the "Query" window in Access. Go to the Menu Bar, click on "Query" and then click on "Update Query," as shown in **Figure 9-12.**

Figure 9-12

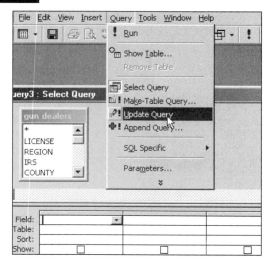

Just as you might go into Microsoft Word or Microsoft Excel and use the "Find and Replace" function to correct the spelling, you use "Update" in Access. The advantage of "Update" is that you can change thousands of records if you need to. You would write this query as in **Figure 9-13.**

Figure 9-13

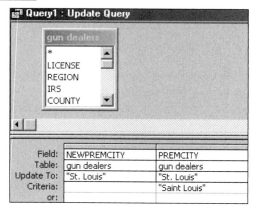

In SQL, you could write it as in **Figure 9-14.** ("Gun dealers" is in brackets because it is two separate words.)

Figure 9-14

> **Query3 : Update Query**
>
> UPDATE [gun dealers]
> SET NEWPREMCITY = "St. Louis"
> WHERE PREMCITY="St Louis" OR PREMCITY= "Saint Louis";

In either case, your data would look like **Figure 9-15.**

Figure 9-15

PREMCITY	NEWPREMCITY
St. Louis	St. Louis
Saint Louis	St. Louis
St Louis	St. Louis

Now, if you wanted to count all the gun dealers in St. Louis, you could write a query that used "NEWPREMCITY" and counted the number of gun dealers. The result is shown in **Figure 9-16.**

Figure 9-16

St. Louis	50

This is only the beginning of data cleaning, but the practice of creating a new field and then putting a standardized spelling in that field is common and necessary.

▼ Header-aches

You finally persuade an agency to give you information in an electronic form rather than on a printout. You get the record layout and **disk,** rush back to your office and transfer the information onto your computer's hard drive. You then browse through the information — and what do you see? A horror show of headers!

Headers are the bits of information that go across the top of a printout page. They may tell you the date, page number and other information that has no place in your database of columns and rows. An example is given in **Figure 9-17.**

Figure 9-17

Date 02/02/93	Administrative Services		Page 3
Name	Town	Zip	Salary
Gerald Sun	Lincoln	06230	20,423
Mary Moon	Jefferson	93914	34,433

In response, the agency — through incompetence, laziness or nastiness — apparently gave you the image of each printed-out page instead of the raw data. Fortunately, you can correct the problem with a word processor, database manager or special software. (We won't go through every step in this handbook, but we'll go over the basic idea of what you can do.)

If you can import the information into a database, you will likely end up with nonsense records at the beginning of each row that starts with "Date." For example, the information might look like what you see in **Figure 9-18.**

Figure 9-18

NAME	TOWN	ZIP	SALARY
Date 02/02/93	Administrative Services	Page 3	
Gerald Sun	Lincoln	06230	20,423
Mary Moon	Jefferson	93914	34,433

But with a "where" statement — such as "delete all records where name like 'Date*'" — you can locate the offending records and eliminate them. With a word processing program or specialized programs, you can eliminate the headers before importing the information into a database. In Access, you would go to the "Query" window, as you did in updating a table, and this time choose "Delete Query." Then you would follow the same process as updating and have a query that looks like **Figure 9-19.**

Figure 9-19

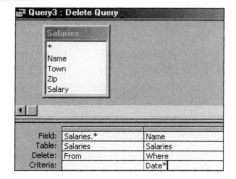

▼ **Mainframe Misery**

Although some journalists have success with **mainframe** computers, most are doing computer-assisted reporting work on personal or Macintosh computers. Yet mainframes — the large computers still used by governments — still exist to frustrate journalists. Not only do mainframes supply a wealth of gibberish languages and practices, they supply bad advice in layouts and bothersome letters. We will share several common examples.

A layout from a mainframe operation often specifies a numeric type of field for ZIP codes and identification numbers. Mainframe software does not have a problem knowing that each digit in those numbers is important. But when you import that information into a database manager on a **PC,** you may face enormous problems. For example, if you tell some database managers to import the ZIP code or identification number into the numeric field, this will cause significant damage. If the database manager sees a ZIP code that begins with a "0," it will eliminate the "0" because it looks meaningless.

Thus, for journalists who work with ZIP codes that begin with "0" (such as 01776), all ZIP codes would be imported as four characters (1776) instead of five. Those ZIP codes will be useless not only for mailing addresses, but also for matching one database to another.

The same disaster can happen with identification codes. An employee with the identification number 042325 in a mainframe will have it rendered as 42325 in a database manager. This is inaccurate and also prevents accurate matches.

The way to escape this peril is to always import ZIP codes, identification numbers and phone numbers into character fields. Generally, import as a character field any number that will never be added, subtracted, multiplied or divided. The database manager then will preserve all the digits.

Fields that contain dates can be another problem. Many journalists split the field into three fields (year, month and day) to make things simpler. Others import the dates into character fields. Cleaning up dates is a problem even for the more advanced CAR practitioners.

Another mainframe misery that haunts journalists is the world of the programming language COBOL. If an agency has a mainframe and uses COBOL — as the Federal Election Commission still does on its downloadable data — it is quite possible that after importing you will get a funny-looking number when you expect to see a dollar amount. Instead of 45222 (as in $452.22), you might get 4522B. In the case of 4522B, you need to somehow append the digit "2" to the number. Moreover, you will have to fix other numbers as well. If there is an "A," that means "1." The letter "F" stands for "6" and so on. Altogether, there are 10 letters, each standing for "0" through "9."

Dealing with this problem involves two strategies you already have encountered. First, when you import the numbers, you want to make the "Hartfor" mistake intentionally. With 4522B, you would create two fields instead of one by truncating the "amount" field. One field — call it "amount" — would contain all numbers up to the letter (in this example, 4522). The second field — call it "letter" — would contain only the "B."

Then you would create another field called "newamount" and write an "Update" statement. The "Update" statement is tricky because you are "appending" a digit, not adding it to the number. You are not adding 2 to 4522. That would give you 4524 — and that's the wrong number.

You want the number to look like 45222. You need to put an extra space in the number by multiplying by 10 and putting the 2 there. So your command would read as follows.

Update newamount with (amount * 10) + 2 for letter = "B"

The "amount * 10" turns 4522 into 45220. Now you can safely add the 2 to get 45222.

Then if you want to convert the number to dollars and cents, you would write this.

Update newamount with newamount * .01

And you have 452.22.

This may seem like a lot of work, but it's good to know. Not only might you face this problem, but the exercise shows you how to think about data and how to clean data. The idea of separating a field into two or more parts is crucial when you get into more complex data cleaning.

▼ Offensive Characters

Databases can contain **offensive characters.** They may be weird-looking, smiling faces or misplaced commas or semicolons. Before importing information into a database, you probably want to get rid of them. Most word processing programs allow you to do this fairly easily.

Microsoft Word allows you to click on "Find and Replace" under the "Edit" button to basically write a "search and destroy" instruction. Say you want to eliminate commas in the data. You would type the comma (,) in the "Find" area of the box and leave the "Replace" area blank. You then click on "Replace All."

There is a fancier way to do this with database programs, using tools called **string functions.** String functions are a powerful but sometimes confusing way to clean data. A *string* is a series of letters or numbers or other symbols, such as commas in a field. A *string function* is a command that allows you to alter data in a field.

For example, a string function can permit you to split a field based on a comma or space in the middle of a field. This can be handy when you are trying to match names in one table with names in another. One table may put the first name in a separate field and the last name in another field. But another table may put the last and first names in the same field, such as "Smith, John." To make the names in the second field useful for a match, you can use the comma as a marker to split the name into a first name and a last name.

This guide does not cover string functions, but the National Institute for Computer-Assisted Reporting has many handouts on this. What's important is that you know this kind of sophisticated data cleaning is possible.

▼ Parsing

Parsing has long been a popular way of doing data cleaning in spreadsheets. **Parsing** means drawing column lines between different kinds of data. One drawback is that spreadsheets can handle only up to 65,000 records. Another is that parsing is somewhat awkward.

But the import wizard you saw in Chapter 2 will look at a text file when you open it and suggest column lines. If the text file is in a tabular format (i.e., it looks like columns), the spreadsheet can rapidly arrange the data. This is especially handy for small files downloaded from online. The spreadsheet enables you to do that easily. You can draw lines between the text columns by clicking. You can delete them by putting the cursor on the line and double-clicking.

Once again, no database is perfect or complete, but that doesn't mean it cannot be made usable.

▼ CAR Wars

▼ The Washington Post series "Deadly Force," which won a Pulitzer Prize, resulted from a close examination of the FBI's Supplementary
▼ Homicide Report. The examination revealed that the SHR data for the country that year did not have a single "81" — the code for a
▼ justifiable homicide by a police officer. Neither did any of the other years I checked.
▼ This suggested that whole records were missing from the dataset. The FBI's own documentation provided another corroborating clue. By comparing the number of records cited on the documentation and the number of records written on the computer tape, it was clear that there were 287 fewer records than there were supposed to be.

After conversations with the FBI, I found that they did collect the data but did not make it part of their "standard release." After two requests, the FBI delivered another computer tape that contained hundreds of "81s." The raw numbers were remarkable. Only officers in a handful of cities — all much larger than Washington, D.C. — had shot and killed more people. Ultimately, these records served as a starting point for the series.

Jo Craven McGinty, formerly of The Washington Post, now at Newsday

Chapter Checklist

- Make sure that identification and ZIP codes contain all numbers.

- Watch for missing words.

- Match the record layout carefully to the actual data.

- Use word processors or string functions in database managers to correct errors.

- Know how many records are supposed to be in the database.

- Use a spreadsheet parsing when the number of records is small.

- Compare total amounts in your database to hard-copy reports.

 # Your Turn to Practice

1 Get part of the Federal Election Commission contributor database or use the database Tenncands.

2 Open your table or the table Tenngive. Copy it as a new table called "Tenngive2." Using the "Design view," create a new field called "occupation2."

3 Copy all the occupations in the occupation field into the "occupation2" field.

4 Using the update command, change all attorneys and lawyers in "occupation2" to lawyers. Then change all doctors and physicians to doctors.

5 Using "occupation2," now group by occupations, and total the amounts of contributions.

> **www**
>
> For more exercises in importing and cleaning data, go to
> **www.ire.org/carbook/chapter9**

CHAPTER 10

Doing the Computer-Assisted Reporting Story

How to Report and Write with Data

> *Computer-assisted reporting is no different than other journalism in an important way: Often the best stories start with a reporter's gut instinct.*
>
> **— David Knox, Akron Beacon-Journal**

You have the computer, the software and the realization that the judicious and skillful use of computer-assisted reporting techniques can create good news stories.

But now what?

If you're not careful, you can suffer a severe case of reporter's block, trying to figure out what stories to do and how to do them. Worse, a large database will swallow you up with its complexities so that you may never finish the story. But stop and think about what you have learned in this book.

First, computer-assisted reporting is an essential part of the newsgathering process. It is not a separate endeavor, but an ever-increasing part of journalism that offers techniques to use and improve your current reporting. It should be applied to topics you are interested in reporting on.

When you consider using a database or databases for a story, you should consider these questions as you learned them in the preceding chapters.

- Are there databases relevant to the story that would help with depth, context or ideas? Has anyone used a database for this kind of story?
- Are the databases available on the Internet? Can they be downloaded in usable formats?
- Which software would be appropriate for analyzing the database? A spreadsheet or database manager? Is the database too large for a spreadsheet? Is the database composed of more than one file?
- If the database is not easily available from a Web site, who keeps the database? Have they ever given it out before? What are the open records laws that govern its use? What is the agency or entity that is releasing the data?
- How could the database be used graphically?
- Who are the people that I will need to profile and interview for this story so that is not a "dry data" story?
- How do I ensure that the story will be fair and not distort or misrepresent the statistics and data that I use?

Perhaps most important is the challenge that goes with all stories. What is the larger question I am seeking to answer with this news story, and will the data help answer that question? You can answer all of these questions with a few key strategies.

▼ Pick a Doable Story

Review stories that have been done at other news organizations and see if you can apply their approach and acquire similar databases to illuminate issues in your area. The resource center at Investigative Reporters and Editors Inc. has thousands of "CAR" stories indexed at its Web site, **www.ire.org/resourcecenter.**

Many of those stories have been entered into the IRE contest and have contest forms that reporters filled out to explain how to do the story, what databases and documents they used and what challenges they faced.

▼ Pick an Available Database

Quite often, journalists spend most of their time acquiring or building a database when doing a computer-assisted reporting story. To avoid that time-consuming process, obtain a database that has been released before, or get a federal database that can be sliced down to the local level. The National Institute for Computer-Assisted Reporting,

www.nicar.org, has more than 40 major federal databases from which the institute can extract the data for your region.

If you are going to build a database, then follow the guidelines in Chapter 8 to avoid getting bogged down in data entry. Keep your first self-built database small and manageable.

▼ Some First-Time Examples

If you want to look at the first stories some reporters did after they learned these techniques, you can check the "first ventures" reported in Uplink, the authoritative newsletter on CAR.

- Jason Callicoat of the South Bend Tribune in Indiana took weather data and parking ticket data for his first try at a computer-assisted reporting story and not only discovered residents weren't likely to get a ticket on a bad weather day, but also that armed forces recruiters owed the city thousands of dollars.
- Edward L. Carter at The Deseret News in Utah produced a story illustrating the lack of females in top management positions at local cities after getting public data on municipal employees, their salaries and other employment information.
- Mark Houser of the Tribune-Review in Pittsburgh used Excel worksheets on lottery sales to help report on high sales to working-class families and other social consequences of Pennsylvania's lottery system.
- Missouri School of Journalism student Mark Greenblatt won an IRE award for using a federal database on the conditions of bridges in Missouri to help him identify deficient and unsafe bridges.

Other reporters have entered data on jury pools or voter registration to turn around stories in just a few days.

▼ Start Small

It once was a matter of pride for a journalist to use a database composed of hundreds of thousands of records. But for many journalists now, some of the most effective stories have come from only a few hundred or thousand records.

Furthermore, starting with a small database allows you to get to know the information. Look for databases that involve only a few columns of names or numbers. If you really have to or want to, you can manually check the database; that will improve your confidence in the information and in your skills.

In the 1980s and early 1990s, most databases came from mainframe computer tapes. They had to be downloaded and broken up into smaller parts to be used on personal computers. Now many databases are already reduced in size at online sites or on disks. For example, some large databases, such as census files, are already broken into small databases in Excel. Journalists now routinely use small census files for stories on housing, income, transportation and ethnic diversity in cities.

▼ Building Your Own

As shown in Chapter 8, it's not that difficult to build your own database. If you build your own database, you immediately take three steps toward a successful story. One, you automatically are familiar with the information because you obtained and organized the data. Two, because data entry is so tedious, you will limit the amount of information and keep it relevant. Three, if *you* had to build a database, then no one else has it, and you may uncover an exclusive story. Remember that a database doesn't have to have thousands or even hundreds of records. Two of the most useful databases I built each had fewer than 150 records.

Karl Idsvoog and Corky Johnson, both broadcast reporters, set a standard in the early 1990s when they showed how effective building a database can be. Their databases resulted in sharp investigative stories, including pieces on the sale of salvaged cars, absenteeism at a county office and wasteful practices at a local housing agency.

At The Hartford Courant, environmental writer Daniel Jones, researcher Leah Segal and I built an abbreviated database on emissions of toxic chemicals by manufacturers after we learned that we would have to wait nine months for government officials to release their database. By doing so, we learned a lot about how companies filled out the hard-copy reports, and we learned that the state had not mentioned 20 percent of the emissions in its reports because of administrative decisions. No one else had the information for months, and we used the database for several exclusive stories.

▼ Match the Database to Your Knowledge

Although electronic databases permit you to learn and to explore new subjects, it's better to get a database on something you know about when you are starting. Building your own database is one way to be sure of the information and how to use it; getting a database on a topic you know about and cover is another way.

A database is a mirror of reality, but a mirror always has flaws. You need to know how bad the flaws are and how distorted the image is. That's why it's good to get a database about your own beat or specialty, and there are numerous databases available online and offline on every beat. The database can highlight problems or provide tips about the subject, but you know the context.

If you find flaws in the database, you have to decide whether it is worth cleaning up those flaws and how long that will take. Some databases simply can't be used without some cleanup, and you must make an assessment of the time and effort that will take before embarking on the work. If it is a matter of standardizing a location name, then it will be easy to do. If it's a matter of parsing one column into three columns, it may take more time.

If you aren't reporting on a familiar subject, then team up with a reporter who does know it. When I worked on a judicial story, I worked with the court reporter. On other subjects, I worked with the environmental reporter, the medical reporter, the city hall reporters or the political reporters. They pointed out problems in the databases and could also discern patterns and clues in them.

▼ The Minimum Story

When you are starting out, never get a database without thinking what the minimum story is. By "minimum story" I mean the surest, most basic story available. After hearing this from legendary investigative editor Robert W. Greene, veteran journalists have taught this approach for all kinds of reporting.

If you get a database of governmental salaries, you can be pretty sure that you will have a story about the average, the median and who gets the highest and lowest. If you get a database of housing prices over the past few years, you can be confident that you will have a story about changes and trends. If you get a database on crime, you will undoubtedly be able to report on the increases and decreases. If you get a database on political contributions, you will have a story about who gave the least and most, and where the contributors were from.

These are minimum stories. They don't always become the lead story of the day, but they are solid and enable you to do meaningful journalism. They also provide you with a foundation of databases that can bolster later stories or can be combined with new databases for even better stories. In addition, they show potential sources that you may be interested in about the topic.

▼ Keep Up with Other Reporters' Work

Too many journalists get caught up in the argument that a story has been done before. Frankly, most stories *have* been done before. That's not the point. The real questions are whether your story is a good one, whether the previous stories have been done thoroughly and correctly and whether your material is worthwhile in the geographic area in which you work.

The same applies to using databases. After all, a reporter in one community can do a reasonably good overview of who deals guns in that community. Possibly there is no shattering news, just an interesting look at the issue. But you may get the same database for your own community and find that many gun dealers are police officers and that some of them sell guns to convicted felons. It's the quality of the database and what you do with it that count.

Therefore, try to keep up with what other journalists are doing. When you read or hear about a journalist who has used a database or online resource that you may be interested in, review the stories to determine how the source might be applicable in your own situation. You also can call (or e-mail) the journalist for tips on the database.

The National Institute for Computer-Assisted Reporting and Investigative Reporters and Editors offer many resources on how journalists have done computer-assisted reporting stories and what databases and software they used. NICAR's listserv, nicar-l, its Web site and the bimonthly newsletter Uplink also give how-to information on computer-assisted reporting.

▼ Integrate Databases into Your Daily Work

Although some journalists do only long projects with databases, you should try to integrate their use into stories on the beat and on the deadline. Indeed, Pat Stith, a veteran investigative reporter at the News & Observer in Raleigh and a leader there in computer-assisted reporting, gave a good tip when he said, "We are going to use databases to create or improve everyday front-page stories and second fronts."

The "improve" part of that statement is especially useful for a journalist beginning to explore computer-assisted reporting. Quietly improve your stories by adding online searches, small spreadsheet calculations and summary data from database managers. You will be able to increase your expertise without unduly increasing expectations within the news organization. And, of course, you will bring depth and context to your daily and beat reporting that will make every story more important and more informative.

▼ Find a Partner

If at all possible, find a partner to learn with. With any new way of thinking and looking at information, it helps to have someone to talk to and discuss solutions to problems. The "buddy system" keeps you focused and also helps prevent errors. Having a friendly colleague look over your shoulder when you are doing your first queries or calculations will save you a lot of time and trouble. You will also learn faster by helping someone else.

▼ Become Familiar with Data Processing

Because you are learning a new subject, take the time to read some magazines about computer hardware and software. Reviews of hardware and software may be difficult to understand, but they can help you learn the language and find tools that might help you do a better job.

You should also get to know people who work in the computer field but who are not journalists themselves. They often have a quick answer for a problem that has baffled you and other journalists.

Listservs on software, social research methods and public databases are full of helpful how-to tips and story ideas.

▼ Look for Tips

Keep a narrow focus when you start doing these kinds of stories, but don't overlook potentially good stories or tips in databases. When you have finished your minimum story, set aside a half hour to peruse a database. (Make that a firm half hour by using a timer, or you could pass half a day without realizing it.)

Look for tips by searching for particular words, by looking for "outliers," by creating summary data using "Group By," by doing percentages or by just scanning the databases for trends and patterns. Often, a good story can emerge from a scan of a database.

▼ Writing the Story

Too often, when starting to write the story, reporters let themselves become overwhelmed by the statistics and numbers. You can't write your notebook, as has often been said.

Throughout the reporting process — especially when dealing with data, numbers and statistics — you need to think about summarizing. As Sarah Cohen of The Washington Post has said, "Which is the one most important number that tells the story?" Is it a raw number like 5,000? Is it a rate, ratio or percentage increase?

If possible, the key number should be the only number in the first 10 paragraphs of a story. Most likely, you will have other numbers, but many of them should be visualized in a chart or graph or map. Otherwise, the reader or viewer will be overwhelmed. If you think it will provide a service, then list all the numbers on a Web site.

Once you have the number, what is the best human example you have of it? If you lead a story with an anecdote about one case, it should represent the pattern or outliers you found in the data.

Sometimes, in complex stories you need to explain how you did the story and what data you used. Many journalists use what journalist Pat Stith first called a "nerd box." In that box, separate from the main story, you can provide details on methodology and data that give your story more credibility.

In addition, you need to get out and see what you are writing about. If it is toxic dumps, then go look at them. If it is schools, then visit them. If it is small businesses, go there and do interviews. It is key that if you do the lab (CAR) work, you also do the fieldwork and the legwork. Remember that good stories are about people and for people.

▼ Good Reporting and Ethics

Throughout your newsgathering and data work, remember to be accurate and fair. There are plenty of politicians, researchers and advocates who want much too badly to find numbers that will back up their positions. As an independent journalist, it is your job not only to expose their manipulation of numbers, but also to prevent yourself from seeing what you hope to see.

Quite often, the story is even a better one if the database doesn't support your initial hypothesis. But the only good story is one that summarizes accurately what you have found. In addition, you need to be willing to share the highlights of your findings during your interviews and to listen and consider the criticism. It is much better to find out you are wrong before you publish or air a story than after the public sees it. In addition, you need to constantly think of the "lurking variables" as you do your story — that is, what other factors could cause the data to look the way you are seeing it.

Throughout our bail story, Jack Ewing and I constantly tried to play "devil's advocate" with the data and to come up with arguments against our initial findings. Push your editor or colleagues to look at your work critically.

When the story is complete, go back and check your facts line by line. Whenever possible, tie them back to your data and documents.

▼ Stay Curious, Get Excited

Last, stay curious and excited about your stories. The lasting attraction of computer-assisted reporting is that you can do stories you never could have done before in ways you never thought of. Moreover, you can be creative and responsible at the same time and provide the public with the best and most accurate view of an issue.

▼ Reporting with CAR

Here is a summary of the steps in doing CAR stories.

I. Begin the story with a hypothesis or question.
   A. You get a tip from a person.
   B. Grouping and sorting data you already have shows possible trends, patterns or unusual events.
II. Draw up a list of people to interview, places to visit and databases and documents to analyze.
   A. People can include experts, agencies, community members and the custodians and users of relevant data.
   B. Places include agencies, neighborhoods or sites that the data will refer to.
   C. Databases are those that already are created or those you may have to build from documents or observations. You will need to decide what software and hardware you will need for them.
III. Prioritize your list and compose a schedule for completing the list.
   A. All open records requests should be made as early as possible.
   B. Plan to interview certain people — usually administrators — at the beginning of your work and then interview the same people after your site visits, data analysis and other interviews.
   C. Do the data analysis. Look for flaws in the data and your methods.
   D. You may need to do your site visits before the data analysis and after the data analysis. Data analysis will help you focus.
   E. You need to take into account that your list may grow and you will need to redo your schedule.

IV. Write the story.
A. Summarize your data work and decide what are the key numbers and what should go into graphics or nerd boxes.
B. Summarize your interviews and site visits and decide who and what is most representative of your reporting and data analysis.
C. Check your data findings against outside reports based on the data, and run your findings past experts or persons familiar with the data.
D. Outline the story and decide on the appropriate tone.
E. Be prepared to reinterview some people and to redo your data analysis as part of the verification process.
F. Write the story.
G. Do a line-by-line check of the story.
H. Be prepared to defend your methodology.
I. Plan your possible follow-up stories before you publish or air.

▼ CAR Wars

▼ After taking a NICAR boot camp, it wasn't long before I was finding ways to use my newfound skill.

▼ In fact, CAR has become an everyday method for me. When I'm looking for information, among the first things I ask is "How are the records kept?" or "How far back do those records date?" The whole process is always an adventure.

▼ For one story, an initial tip on missing school equipment came from a source in the fixed assets department. We then requested from the school an inventory of missing equipment.

They declined to give it to us electronically and instead supplied the list on paper. The list totaled $2.5 million of equipment lost over a five-year period. I entered all the information on an Excel spreadsheet, added up the totals, calculated percentage increase/loss over time, sorted the data to see which schools were losing the most and looked at the items that were lost the most frequently. The list included VCRs, computers, televisions and band equipment. Two of the most unusual items were a John Deere tractor and a walk-in freezer. Our story created quite a stir, and a subsequent audit by the school district revealed that the problem was even worse than we reported: $4.2 million in equipment was missing!

Joe Ellis, KMOL-TV

Chapter Checklist

- Start with small databases.

- Build your own database.

- Get databases for subjects you know.

- Look at how other CAR stories were done.

- Integrate computer-assisted reporting into your daily journalism.

- Use the buddy system.

- Use databases as tipsters.

Hint: The National Institute for Computer-Assisted Reporting has publications on CAR stories and how they were done.

Your Turn to Practice

1 Research the IRE Resource Center at **www.ire.org/resourcecenter** for computer-assisted stories that have been done.

2 Read the last six issues of Uplink.

3 Download three Excel worksheets from the Census Bureau that have information on topics you are interested in.

4 Get a local slice of data (make sure it is in one table) from the IRE and NICAR data library on infrastructure or transportation accidents in your region, and analyze that data.

> **www**
> For more exercises in downloading and importing, go to
> **www.ire.org/carbook/chapter10**

PROFESSIONAL'S APPENDIX A

Choosing Hardware and Software

Choosing the right hardware and software for computer-assisted reporting can be difficult because improvements to these come monthly, if not weekly. Therefore, you need to answer the following questions.

- What kind of spreadsheets and databases do I intend to research or analyze?
- What software do I need to perform that analysis?
- What kind of hardware do I need to run the software, and how much space on the computer do I need?
- What software do I know how to use and for what do I need training?

If you plan to crunch numbers, analyze large databases and go online, then you can quickly identify the software you need. At a minimum, you will need a database manager, a spreadsheet and online software. The storage and **memory** requirements of the software will guide you in your selection of hardware. If you are going to do statistics or mapping, you need the most hard drive space and random access memory (RAM) you can get.

Also, find out what kind of software your colleagues are using. You may want to choose their preferred brands because if they are familiar with that software, they can help you learn it or discuss problems you encounter when using the software.

For most database manager software now on the market, you will need at least 10 to 20 gigabytes on your hard drive and 256 megabytes or more of **RAM.** Get as much RAM as possible, since memory is crucial to effectively running software programs.

Your processor, if IBM-compatible, should be the fastest processor you can afford. (The higher the gigahertz, the faster it goes.) If you are using a Macintosh, you should choose one with the highest-speed chip. Try to get as fast a connection as you can to the Internet; a broadband or cable connection leaves the modem speeds in the dust. Last, because of the graphics in software, a 17-inch color monitor is a must on a desktop computer and as large a one as you can get for a laptop.

Here is a sample of minimum laptop specifications as of 2003:

- 20-gigabyte hard drive
- 1.8-gigahertz processing chip
- 256 megabytes of random access memory
- 14.5" screen
- DVD-ROM reader
- 3.5" floppy drive
- Ethernet card
- 56K modem

For the Internet, almost every day a new provider releases new software. Netscape Communications Corp.'s software or Microsoft Explorer are the ones used most often. For other software, journalists frequently use the following spreadsheets: Microsoft Excel, Quattro Pro for Windows and Lotus 1-2-3. They frequently use the following database managers: Microsoft Access, Microsoft Visual FoxPro and Paradox for Windows. In the Mac environment, they use Filemaker Pro or Visual FoxPro.

In statistical software, the two most popular are SPSS (Statistical Software for the Political and Social Sciences) and SAS (Statistical Analysis System), which are produced by the SAS Institute in Cary, NC.

Journalists using mapping software gravitate toward ArcView, produced by ESRI, which can be found at **www.esri.com.**

To keep up with hardware and software changes, prices and quality, read commercial computer magazines such as Computer Shopper, PC Magazine, PC Computing or any others on the magazine stand that look helpful. For additional and more specific tips, subscribe to the NICAR listserv, nicar-l, by going to **http://www.ire.org/membership/ listserv.html.**

PROFESSIONAL'S APPENDIX **B**
A Short Introduction to Statistical Software

In the last decade, more journalists have begun using some of the methods and statistical analysis techniques of social scientists. But if numbers and spreadsheets make journalists uncomfortable, the subject of statistics generates outright terror. Nonetheless, journalists report on statistics every day with a partial understanding, and they avoid statistics even though using a few of the basic analytic skills could give them good clues and directions about a story. Yet, as journalists become more computer-savvy, they can also become more number-savvy. And as they become more number-savvy, they become more statistics-savvy. Journalists constantly compare and measure, and statistics — as social science researchers have long shown — provide good tools for doing just that.

The necessity of acquiring basic statistical skills is becoming important for journalists who want to flourish in the 21st century. "Statistics are used or misused even by people who tell us, 'I don't believe in statistics,' then claim that all of us or most people or many do such and such," wrote journalist Victor Cohn in his excellent book "News and Numbers." "The question for reporters is, how should we not merely repeat such numbers, stated or implied, but also interpret them to deliver the best possible picture of reality?"

Philip Meyer, a veteran reporter and pioneer in the computer-assisted field, says in his book "Precision Journalism," "They are raising the ante on what it takes to be a journalist." Meyer, who teaches at the University of North Carolina, has used social science research methods for years in his consulting work for news organizations.

This appendix examines a few basic descriptive statistics and extends the skills and ways of thinking we discussed in the chapters on spreadsheets. Consider this a prelude to reading in-depth books such as Meyer's, Cohn's and Sarah Cohen's "Numbers in the Newsroom" and also taking courses in social science statistics.

But note that a journalist, or anyone with a little knowledge of statistics, can be dangerous. Social science researchers have become concerned about journalists misinterpreting and misusing statistical methods — not through malice but through ignorance. Journalists using social science research methods should be braced for continuing debate over the numbers and interpretations after a story appears.

Statistics introduced at this level should serve as safeguards. They should not make journalists leap to conclusions, but they should prompt journalists to question the veracity of their own hypotheses and generalizations and those of the people the journalists are covering.

▼ Software and Analysis

SPSS and SAS are the two most frequently used statistical software. Both allow you to do basic analysis in an immediate and practical way. The basic tools are frequencies, crosstabs, graphing and recoding.

Using frequencies in statistical software allows you in only one step to count your records and calculate the percentage of the total those counts make.

Many journalists first cut their statistical teeth on an annual home mortgage loan database from the Federal Reserve. The database, created by the Home Mortgage Disclosure Act, contains information on applications including ethnicity, income and action.

Figure B-1 shows a slice of 10,802 records on loan applicants from part of Tennessee. (Records have been simplified and ethnicity changed from coded numbers to black and white.)

Figure B-1

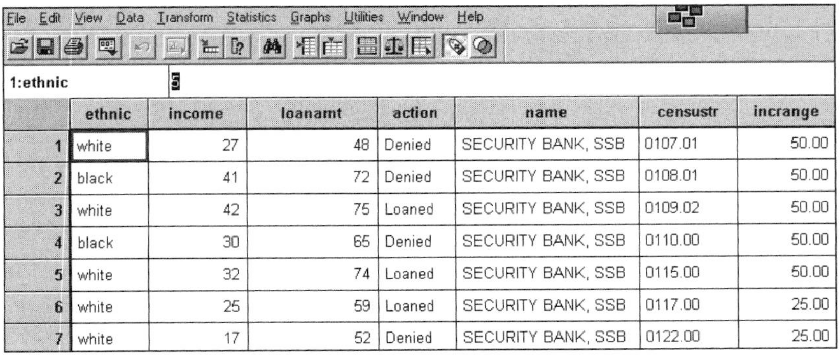

File Edit View Data Transform Statistics Graphs Utilities Window Help

1:ethnic

	ethnic	income	loanamt	action	name	censustr	incrange
1	white	27	48	Denied	SECURITY BANK, SSB	0107.01	50.00
2	black	41	72	Denied	SECURITY BANK, SSB	0108.01	50.00
3	white	42	75	Loaned	SECURITY BANK, SSB	0109.02	50.00
4	black	30	65	Denied	SECURITY BANK, SSB	0110.00	50.00
5	white	32	74	Loaned	SECURITY BANK, SSB	0115.00	50.00
6	white	25	59	Loaned	SECURITY BANK, SSB	0117.00	25.00
7	white	17	52	Denied	SECURITY BANK, SSB	0122.00	25.00

"Ethnic" is the ethnicity of the applicant, and "result" is the action taken by the financial institution. The monetary amounts are given in thousands, so "50" is actually $50,000. In **Figure B-1,** you are looking at data in SPSS. Although you are looking at statistical software, you are still in the two-dimensional world of columns and rows. But the language is different. In statistical software, the columns are called **"variables"** and the rows are called "observations."

With this data, you might want to get an idea of how many loan applicants are black, Hispanic or white. This concept is the same as "Group by" in the chapters on databases, but in statistical software you can get not only a count of each ethnicity, but also a percentage.

First, go to the Menu Bar and click on "Statistics," then on "Summarize" and then on "Frequencies," as shown in **Figure B-2.**

Figure B-2

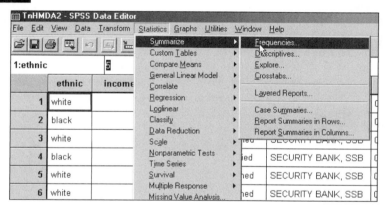

When you click on "Frequencies," you see a screen like the one in **Figure B-3.**

Figure B-3

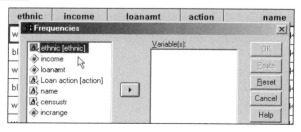

This screen allows you to choose the variable that you want to count. In this case, it is "ethnic." To move "ethnic" from the box on the left to the Variable(s) box, click on "ethnic" and then click on the arrow between the boxes. The result is shown in **Figure B-4.**

Figure B-4

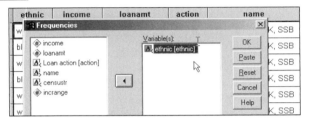

Once you have selected "ethnic," click on "OK." In **Figure B-5** you see the result. SPSS has counted each ethnicity and given the percentage of the total in the first two columns. The "Frequencies" column is the actual count of each record for an applicant. (By the way, SPSS also tells you that there is an ethnicity for each applicant because there are no "Missing Cases.")

Figure B-5

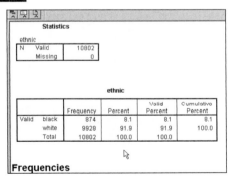

You can see from **Figure B-5** that most of the applicants are white. Although the number of black applicants is relatively small, you see that there probably are enough black applicants in this database for you to continue your analysis of whether there is racial disparity. For example, if there were only 20 or 30, it would be difficult to justify a comparison to white applicants.

▼ Descriptive Statistics

The next step in exploring the database might be to get an idea of the averages of loan amount and income. Once again, go to "Statistics," then "Summarize," but then choose "Descriptives," as shown in **Figure B-6.**

Figure B-6

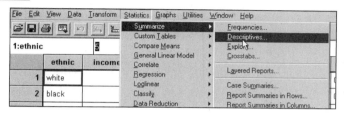

This will allow you to find the averages on applicants' loan amounts and incomes. At the same time, you might want to know what the lowest and highest amounts are and what the standard deviation (or "spread" around the average) looks like. Standard deviation, in this case, indicates how closely the loan amounts gather around the average. If the standard deviation is larger than the average, it means there aren't many individual loans that are "average," but there are groups of amounts on either side of the average.

In **Figure B-7,** you find two columns are numeric, which means you can do calculations on them.

Figure B-7

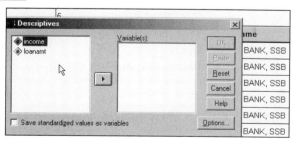

Move "loanamt" and "income" to the Variable(s) box by clicking on each one and then on the arrow between the two boxes. Then click on "Options" (see **Figure B-8**) at the bottom of the screen to decide what kinds of calculations you want.

Figure B-8

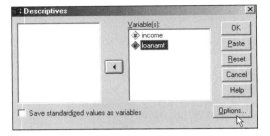

The software gives you several choices. You should choose mean, minimum, maximum and standard deviation (see **Figure B-9**) because these measurements will give you a quick look at the numbers. Mean is average, minimum is the minimum number and maximum is the maximum number.

Figure B-9

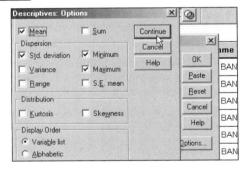

Hit "Continue," then "OK" and return to the original screen, where you hit "OK" again. The results are shown in **Figure B-10.**

Figure B-10

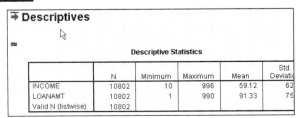

➡ **Descriptives**

Descriptive Statistics

	N	Minimum	Maximum	Mean	Std. Deviation
INCOME	10802	10	996	59.12	62
LOANAMT	10802	1	990	91.33	75
Valid N (listwise)	10802				

You can see that the average income is $59,120, the minimum income is $10,000 and the maximum income is $996,000. For amount of loans the average is $91,330, the minimum is $1,000 and the maximum is $990,000. The standard deviations are $62,820 for income (which means there aren't a lot of incomes around the average) and $75,760 for loan amounts (which means most of the individual loan amounts tend to gather around the average).

This look at the database tells you that you have some potential outliers. The $1,000 figure could be data-entry errors or special cases, which means that you will need to call the source of the data to fact-check the database. The high loan amounts and incomes (indicated by maximum) are probably numbers that you want to throw out when making comparisons; there are so few of them and they could distort your results.

There is a handy tool called a "histogram" that lets you visualize how the data are distributed. It's found under "Graphs" in the SPSS menu and is not too difficult to use. Here's a look at the histogram for income in **Figure B-11.** Notice that there are far fewer salaries on the right, where the amounts are high. The left side of the histogram is the number of incomes, whereas the numbers along the bottom are the actual income amounts. Note that the most number of incomes are not around the $59,000 average, but gather more around $20,000.

Figure B-11

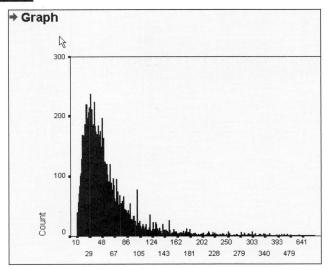

▼ Crosstabs

Now you want to get closer to the hypothesis of the story: How do denial rates compare among the races? Remember that the database on home mortgages was created to analyze the treatment of different races seeking loans and to help prevent disparity. So we ask, "What percentage of blacks are turned down as compared to percentage of whites?"

Another quick way to get started in statistical software is through crosstabs. Crosstabs, which are like an extension of frequencies, permit a journalist to get an overall view of data in several ways. A crosstab, like a pivot table, allows you to compare or look at the associations between different categories of information (or "variables," as they are called in statistical software).

When you set up a crosstab of two variables, for example, you should think about what is the "cause" variable and what is the "effect" variable, although social researchers don't call them that. They call them the "independent" variable and the "dependent" variable. In this case, does whether someone gets a loan depend on the color of someone's skin?

Generally, journalists put the independent variable in the column and the dependent variable in the row. In analyzing whether a person might be denied a home loan on the basis of ethnicity, ethnicity is the independent variable and the result of the home loan application is the dependent variable. That is, does one's success in obtaining a loan depend on one's ethnic background?

As usual, it's easier to show this than to explain it. In this example, the focus is on home loans in the Nashville, Tennessee, area in the 1990s. The database has been altered to make it easier to understand because the data came with ethnicity and action of financial institutions in numeric codes. SPSS allows you to convert those codes into words fairly easily. Also, only blacks and whites will be compared.

Figure B-12 shows how to get going. Go back to "Statistics," then "Summarize" and then "Crosstabs."

Figure B-12

After you click on "Crosstabs," you will get a familiar screen that gives you choices of variables to use. You choose "ethnic" as the independent variable, so you put it in the Column(s) box. You then put "Loan action" — the action that could be dependent on ethnicity — in the Row(s) box (see **Figure B-13**).

Figure B-13

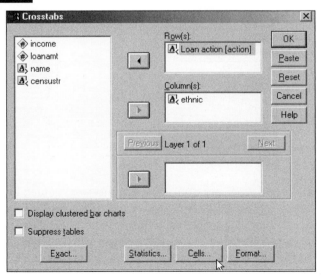

At the bottom of the screen will be several choices. Click on "Cells," as shown by the cursor in **Figure B-13,** and you will see more choices, as shown in **Figure B-14.**

Figure B-14

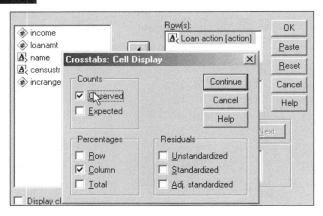

Clicking on "Column" will give you percentages of denials of loans for each ethnic group. Return to the main screen by clicking on "Continue" and "OK." You will see a display as shown in **Figure B-15.**

Figure B-15

Loan action * ethnic Crosstabulation					
			ethnic		
			black	white	Total
Loan action	Loaned	Count	399	6205	6604
		% within ethnic	45.7%	62.5%	61.1%
	Approved	Count	67	990	1057
		% within ethnic	7.7%	10.0%	9.8%
	Denied	Count	408	2733	3141
		% within ethnic	46.7%	27.5%	29.1%
Total		Count	874	9928	10802
		% within ethnic	100.0%	100.0%	100.0%

As you can see, 46.7 percent of black applicants were denied loans, whereas 27.5 percent of whites were denied loans. But now you may remember the income differences from one of your descriptive statistics and wonder if there is a way to look at differences with incomes. There is.

Statistical software allows you to routinely create ranges of such things as income. Here's how. Click on "Transform," then "Recode" and then "Into Different Variables," as shown in **Figure B-16.**

Figure B-16

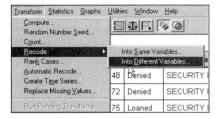

This may seem a little complicated at first, but if you go slowly, it will make sense. **Figure B-17** shows that you click on "income" as the numeric variable containing the information you want to consolidate into ranges. Then type "incrange" as the output variable. This is the name of a new column you will create. Then click on the "Change" button and then on "Old and New Values."

Figure B-17

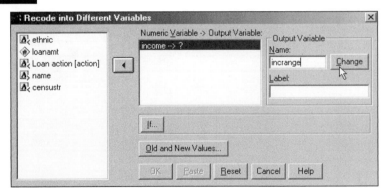

As shown in **Figure B-18,** you can start transforming ranges of incomes into one number. You click on the "Range" button under "Old Value," type "1 through 25," and type "25" under "New Value" and click "Add." That means the number 25 will stand for incomes $1,000 through $25,000. **Figure B-18** shows that you return to the "Range" button after you create the first range and type "26 through 50" to create a second range. You follow this procedure to 150. This means that you will divide the incomes into six groups and rid your calculations of the most extreme "outliers."

Figure B-18

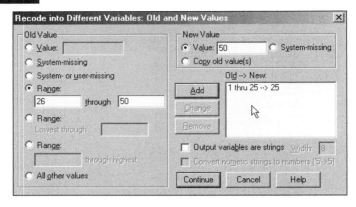

Once those are complete, you click on "Continue" and return to the previous screen and click on "OK." Your revised database with its new column is shown in **Figure B-19.**

Figure B-19

1:incrange		50					
	ethnic	income	loanamt	action	name	censustr	incrange
1	white	27	48	Denied	SECURITY BANK, SSB	0107.01	50.00
2	black	41	72	Denied	SECURITY BANK, SSB	0108.01	50.00
3	white	42	75	Loaned	SECURITY BANK, SSB	0109.02	50.00
4	black	30	65	Denied	SECURITY BANK, SSB	0110.00	50.00
5	white	32	74	Loaned	SECURITY BANK, SSB	0115.00	50.00

Now you can do another crosstab, but you'll need to add one more element. Instead of having just two variables, "incrange" and "result," you will put "ethnic" in the third box, which will allow you to separate out the income ranges and results into crosstabs for each ethnic group. This is known as "controlling" for ethnicity (see **Figure B-20**).

Figure B-20

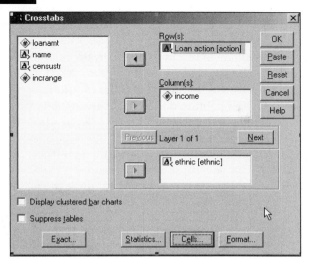

Don't forget to click on "Cells" and pick "Columns" so that you obtain the percentage. Then return to the screen shown in **Figure B-20** and click on "OK." The results for blacks and whites appear in **Figure B-21.**

Figure B-21

Loan action * INCRANGE * ethnic Crosstabulation									
				INCRANGE					
ethnic				25.00	50.00	75.00	100.00	125.00	150.00
black	Loan action	Loaned	Count	82	174	81	26	16	8
			% within INCRANGE	36.1%	43.4%	52.3%	61.9%	66.7%	72.7%
		Approved	Count	17	27	18	2	2	
			% within INCRANGE	7.5%	6.7%	11.6%	4.8%	8.3%	
		Denied	Count	128	200	56	14	6	3
			% within INCRANGE	56.4%	49.9%	36.1%	33.3%	25.0%	27.3%
	Total		Count	227	401	155	42	24	11
			% within INCRANGE	100.0%	100.0%	100.0%	100.0%	100.0%	100.0%
white	Loan action	Loaned	Count	767	2351	1423	747	284	199
			% within INCRANGE	41.5%	57.6%	72.2%	80.6%	79.8%	81.6%
		Approved	Count	209	435	184	78	30	20
			% within INCRANGE	11.3%	10.7%	9.3%	8.4%	8.4%	8.2%
		Denied	Count	871	1293	364	102	42	25
			% within INCRANGE	47.2%	31.7%	18.5%	11.0%	11.8%	10.2%
	Total		Count	1847	4079	1971	927	356	244
			% within INCRANGE	100.0%	100.0%	100.0%	100.0%	100.0%	100.0%

Focus on the applicants whose incomes range from $26,000 to $50,000 and from $51,000 to $75,000. You will see that the denial rates are 49.9 percent and 36.1 percent, respectively, for blacks. As you can see, the equivalent denial percentages for whites are 31.7 percent and 18.5 percent. The denial rate of blacks to whites in the middle class still ranges from 1.5 to 1 to 2 to 1. (That is, 49.9 percent over 31.7 percent is 1.5 to 1, and 36.1 percent over 18.5 percent is nearly 2 to 1.)

At this point, you have established that blacks are denied loans more often than whites — sometimes by a 2 to 1 ratio — even when incomes are in the same range. That's a start for further inquiry into why this has happened. Is it an outcome of race or is it something else?

Perhaps you should compare those applying for loans with the general population in the area. Or perhaps you should examine the reasons for denial. Was there a problem with creditworthiness or the total net worth of the applicants, or some other factor such as location of the home? These are all factors that Philip Meyer refers to as "lurking variables" — factors that may account for differences that you don't recognize immediately.

You've gotten to a point where the reporting really begins, and you are starting with much more knowledge. You have been able to test a hypothesis and get results. The results can be a story idea, or they can verify or dispute someone else's work. Previously you would have waited for a report and then done interviews. Now you can write the rough draft of a report and begin a much more in-depth look at what is happening through interviews, comparisons to other studies and more analysis.

A Short Introduction to Mapping Data

Mapping data is taking columns and rows of information and overlaying that information over geographical maps. By doing this, you can quickly visualize for yourself and readers and viewers what the data mean. For example, using mapping software you can place dots that represent the location of auto accidents on a map of streets, and suddenly a list of accidents turns into clusters of dots at certain intersections and you can see where the dangerous intersections are. In this appendix, we look at the uses of mapping software and some of the techniques you can employ to visualize your data.

There are plenty of examples now in journalism because the mapping of data has quickly gone from the occasional to routine in the past few years for the advanced users of computer-assisted reporting.

You could see how mainstream mapping had become when after the 2000 presidential election, talk show hosts used a map from USA Today from which to spin off jokes. The map, in red and blue, showed that Democratic candidate Al Gore took the urban areas and the eventual winner, Republican George W. Bush, received his votes from the middle of the country and in less populated areas. Comedian Chris Rock suggested, for example, that Bush won the Rockies because no one lives there.

In the early 1990s, a few journalists began making revealing displays of data with mapping software. When Hurricane Andrew hit Florida in 1992, the damage was enormous and costly. In its aftermath, Miami Herald computer-assisted reporter Steve Doig created a map that overlaid wind speed reports over 60,000 building inspection damage reports. The visual result was stunning.

A reporter would expect to find that areas that experienced high wind speeds would have severe building damage and areas with lower wind speeds would have less damage. But Doig's map showed that some areas with lower wind speeds had a lot of damage. The map prompted Doig and other Herald reporters to start their investigation into poor building and inspection practices, particularly those done after 1980. Their work ultimately led to an exposé of incompetence and corruption that won the Herald a Pulitzer Prize.

In mapping, data on a topic such as wind speeds are imported into the software, and as in a database manager, key fields in the table on wind speeds such as longitude and latitude are matched to longitude and latitude in a template table. "Mapping is just such a quick and useful way of taking what could be an otherwise unintelligible pile of information and finding the patterns in it," Doig said.

Doig's and others' ventures inspired hundreds of stories that benefited from the power of mapping during the past decade. As the software has become less expensive and easier to use, reporters throughout the country have used mapping to reveal patterns of drunken driving violations, bank and insurance discrimination, landslides, migration, environmental hazards, lottery sales, school test scores, blighted buildings, health problems, white flight and bad bridges and dams.

In particular, the mapping of census data has become an everyday event. After the 2000 U.S. Census was released, Gary Lenton of The Patriot-News in Harrisburg, Pennsylvania, looked at median incomes to spotlight areas of poverty in Cumberland County. Jeff Claassen of the Fort Worth Star-Telegram tracked commuting times from the census data and discovered that people in low-income neighborhoods had the longest and earliest commutes. Ron Campbell of The Orange County Register in California used census data in mapping software to show the prevalence of Spanish-speaking people in certain neighborhoods in a story that explored the cross-cultural experience in that area.

▼ Turning Matching Sideways

The major concept in mapping is the same one you encounter in database managers: matching. In Chapter 6, we represented matching with the visual interface in Microsoft Access. With mapping software, you are putting one layer of data on top of another instead of drawing lines between fields.

But, as is appropriate with mapping, let's illustrate how to do it. The software we are using in the following examples is ArcView, a relatively inexpensive piece of mapping software. ArcView has become popular because of its friendly interface and because there are many free maps available on the Internet that work in ArcView.

You start with the idea of what your "template" map will be. In this example, we want to look at population change from 1990 to 2000 in the counties of Missouri. ArcView comes with various, premade maps of counties, rivers, streets, other data of geographic locations and some population data. When you open up ArcMap, which is the part of the software that does the actual visualizing, you can choose from existing maps, as shown in **Figure C-1.**

Figure C-1

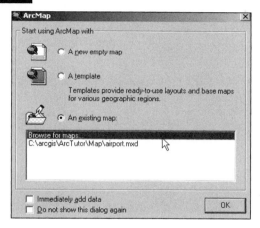

You can choose a map that shows you all the counties in the United States, as in **Figure C-2.** If you click on the map of counties, you can choose "Open Attribute Table" to see the data that lies behind the map.

Figure C-2

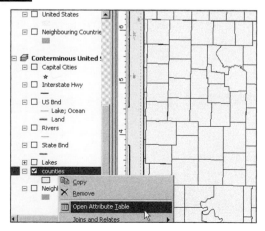

When you open the Attribute Table, you can decide to select counties only in Missouri with a simple formula that the Query Wizard in the software leads you through, as in **Figure C-3.**

Figure C-3

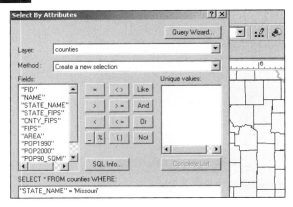

Notice that you are in the world of database managers. The "Fields" are listed at the left. You create a "Query" in "SQL" in the window where you select Missouri. Note that you are using the same "Where" statement you used in Chapter 6.

As a result of the selection, you now can focus on the data for counties in Missouri. You can create new fields and do calculations with the same formulas, just as we did in Chapters 3 and 4 with spreadsheets. For example, we can create a field called "change," which is the difference between 1990 and 2000 populations in each county. We then can do a percentage change by dividing the change by 1990 data in the "Field Calculator" as in **Figure C-4.**

Figure C-4

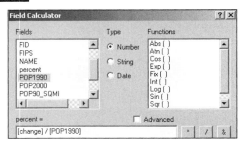

Not only can we do calculations, but we can also sort the data. Thus, we can create a table that shows which Missouri county grew the most from 1990 to 2000, as in **Figure C-5.**

Figure C-5

NAME	perc_chang	change	STATE_NAME
Christian	0.64	20912	Missouri
Stone	0.47	8954	Missouri
Taney	0.42	10736	Missouri
St. Charles	0.36	75839	Missouri
Lincoln	0.35	10020	Missouri
Warren	0.35	6760	Missouri
Cass	0.34	21764	Missouri
Webster	0.29	6988	Missouri
Camden	0.28	7767	Missouri
Benton	0.28	3876	Missouri
Platte	0.27	15341	Missouri
Dallas	0.25	3190	Missouri
Morgan	0.24	3776	Missouri
Barry	0.21	5863	Missouri

From here it is a relatively easy step to divide our data into ranges, as we did in the previous Appendix on Statistical Software (see **Figure C-6**).

Figure C-6

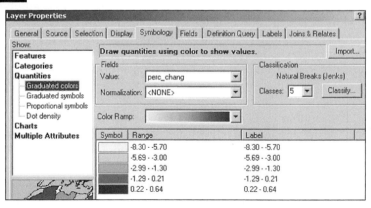

In this example, we let the software choose the five ranges, or classes, of percentage change. It also automatically shades the largest increase in population by percentage change as the darkest shade and the smallest as the lightest. As a result, the map shown in **Figure C-7** is produced, quickly disclosing the largest changes in population.

Figure C-7

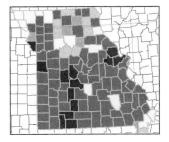

Using basic mapping techniques, Missouri journalists could begin exploring why some counties lost population and why a southernmost county, such as Christian, has had its population leap by 64 percent.

▼ Other Matches

Mapping software can do much more, of course. For example, it can import and match data linked on streets' addresses or latitude and longitude. Matching a table of information to maps can be as easy or as difficult as any enterprising join you might have tried in Chapter 6 on database managers. You don't always get perfect matches. Sometimes the addresses are extremely inconsistent and need cleaning up, and sometimes there are few or no matches.

In this example, we won't go into excruciating detail. (NICAR offers mapping exercises in learning mapping and David Herzog, a Missouri School of Journalism professor, has written a book for ESRI specially tailored for journalists.) But, we will note the essential principles of mapping data.

Pollution from underground storage tanks at gas stations has been an ongoing story throughout the United States. We wanted to look at where these tanks were located in Columbia, Missouri. First, we used an ArcView map to find our county and layered the streets on it. Then we matched our table of storage tanks with the street addresses in Columbia. By searching a state Web site, we found information on storage tanks and leaks, called fac_net.dbf. We were pleased to see a .dbf file because it meant the information is already in a database format and can be used in ArcView. (By the way, the state of Missouri refused to give us a diskette for this table.) To import our table, we clicked on "Tables" in the "View" window and went to a folder that has our storage tank table to add it, as shown in **Figure C-8.**

Figure C-8

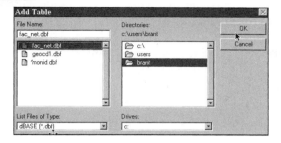

When we looked at the state data, we were happy to see it had street addresses that could be matched to the Columbia street addresses (see **Figure C-9**).

Figure C-9

We could get specific information by clicking on the "Identity" button and clicking on a dot representing a storage tank. After clicking on the "Identity" button, we got information linked to the dot. This was a Wendy's restaurant, as shown in **Figure C-10.**

Figure C-10

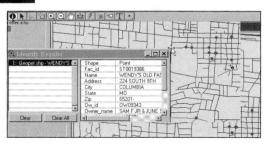

We had no idea of the severity of the problem or the unexpected places that leakage occurred. It turned out that when the gas station closed and the land was sold to a local church, the leaking was only then discovered and cleaned up. There were many other story leads in this data.

In another story, we looked at the location of dams in Boone County, Mo., and the potential danger of them. Using federal data on dams, which is available at NICAR, we matched the dams to their locations in the city by longitude and latitude. Once again, we saw things we didn't know were there. For example, Boone County has many dams that are not easily seen and are in highly populated areas. Some of the dams are aging, and there is no evacuation plan if they begin collapsing. If you look at the information in **Figure C-11,** you will see that the Woodrail Dam has a "high" hazard (it means if it collapses, many people could be injured or killed) and it has "no" EAP (emergency action plan). While the data gives you information, you suddenly see how close a dam really is to a nearby population center when you put it on a map.

Figure C-11

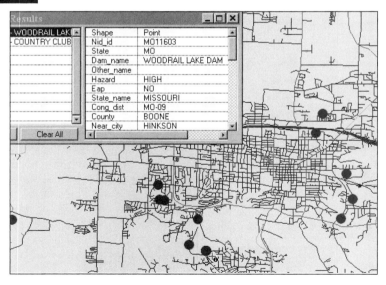

With a database and a map, we suddenly had many tips for a story. With mapping, we can see where the major problems could be. You can then ask for the full inspection paperwork on dams that are old and potentially dangerous. Then you could begin to do interviews of inspectors and officials to see why there are no emergency action plans.

▷ PROFESSIONAL'S APPENDIX **D**

A Short Introduction to Social Network Analysis

Throughout this book, we have looked at the most common approaches to data analyses currently being used by journalists for producing stories. But there is a new approach that journalists have begun to borrow from the social sciences: social network analysis, an approach and a method for the analysis of social structure.

For example, The Washington Post used social network analysis in early 2003 to report on a group of language schools in the Los Angeles area that appeared to be "visa mills" for foreign students. In "INS Moves to Plug Visa Leaks," Post reporters looked into schools that bore little resemblance to real institutions of higher learning. Of a dozen schools visited by the reporters, none had more than a handful of students, and one had no teachers and no staff save for a receptionist.

Using a database of student visas, the newspaper showed that a total of 23 related language schools in the Los Angeles area had accounted for 33,000 visas issued, many good for up to two years.

Finding the relationship between those 23 schools involved a combination of database work, social network analysis, interviews and site visits. At first, simple counting in the database of visas identified several individuals — mostly, but not entirely, in California — who had signed many forms required for student visas on behalf of all kinds of schools, including universities and colleges. Expanding the criteria of the search in the database to include any other person that had signed forms on behalf of those schools eventually created a network of dozens of schools and individuals, loosely linked through their names on the documents. Many were in Los Angeles, and most were language schools.

Using a program designed for network analysis, database editor Sarah Cohen imported the data into software called UCINET, which visualized the relationships. With that, she was able to whittle down the total by removing any school that had only one link to the rest of the network. That left her with 23 schools, all of them language schools in the Los Angeles area.

Cohen said all of her work could have been done using a database manager but that it was much simpler to use UCINET, a tool made for this kind of relationship analysis. It's the same as using Excel because it's easier than using a calculator or using Access because it's easier than making piles of index cards.

▼ Visualizing Relationships

Many other professions already have been using social network analysis for some time. Among the users are business consultants, intelligence and law enforcement agencies, public health investigators, sociologists and anthropologists.

Using free or inexpensive computer software such as UCINET or Pajek, researchers look at social structures such as interlocking boards of directors, neighborhoods or drug use in the inner city. The software and mathematical analysis basically allows the researcher to map relationships and the strength of those relationships and the placement of those relationships in the social structure being looked at.

As Ken Frank, who teaches the topic at Michigan State University, says, "Network analysis is based on the intuitive notion that these patterns are important features of the lives of the individuals who display them. Network analysts believe that how an individual lives depends in large part on how that individual is tied into the larger web of social connections."

The concepts of social network analysis began developing in the 1930s, but it took a big leap ahead when computer graphics became available in the 1970s. Quite often the data used for this approach are survey data. For example, public health researchers in Hartford, CT, tracked and mapped the relationships of who purchased heroin from whom and who injected it together and how race affected use. They gathered the data by surveying heroin users. The survey results were the dataset used in the network analysis.

Journalists and the public became more aware of this kind of analysis following the 2001 terrorist attacks against the World Trade Center. A practitioner of this method, business consultant Valdis E. Krebs quickly outlined the possible relationships and organization of the 19 terrorists involved in the attack. Using open sources — that is, information from newspapers — he was able to visually portray their contacts.

Krebs published an article, "Mapping Networks of Terrorist Cells," on his work in the magazine Connections with his own computer-produced maps of relationships like those shown in **Figure D-1.**

Figure D-1

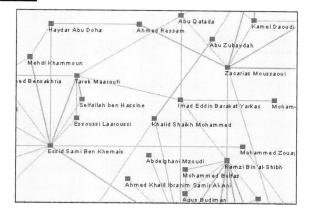

Accompanying this diagram and others were color codes for each of the terrorists noting which airline crash he was involved with. The diagrams showed which terrorist had met with which terrorist according to records in the public purview — newspapers clips and leaks from law enforcement. The diagram showed how infrequent the contacts had been and who belonged to which terrorist cell. It also showed how isolated each cell could be to ensure secrecy.

Krebs noted that further networks to map the terrorists would include a "trust" network using prior contacts in families and neighborhoods and a "money and resources" network based on bank account and money transfer records and credit card use. This is a dramatic example of the use of social network analysis, but it shows the power to visualize relationships, especially in large datasets.

▼ A Different Way to Look at Data

Like the other computer-assisted techniques you have learned, social network analysis has its own language. Two crucial terms are *node* and *line*. In the Krebs illustration, each terrorist would be a node and each relationship a line.

Social network analysis also looks at information differently from traditional columns and rows. Each column is a category of information, and each row is a record — information about one person or occurrence or thing. A fictional list of corporate executives and the corporate boards on which they serve is shown in **Figure D-2.** (This, however, is not the format in which data are imported into analysis software.)

Figure D-2

Name	Title	Company	Board1	Board2	Board3	Board4
Smith	President	EDT	EDT	ABC	LMN	XYZ
Vargas	Treasurer	XYZ	XYZ	ABC	None	None
Jackson	President	ABC	ABC	LMN	EDT	None
Wang	Comptroller	LMN	LMN	ABC	None	None

As you can easily see in this small dataset, some of these executives sit on the board of each other's companies. In recent years, business reporters have delved into questions raised by interlocking directorships and potential conflicts of interest. Social network analysis gives those reporters a chance to find and visualize those relationships created by interlocking boards of directors. But the data need to be rearranged first. In this analysis, we care about the relationships and who knows whom. So we will rearrange the data into what's known as a "sociomatrix" (see **Figure D-3**).

By putting the data into this kind of table, you can see more easily who is on which board and who has the most relationships. The number "1" means they sit on the board of the other person, and "0" means they don't. The X simply notes the person sits on his or her own company board. To actually get the data into a program like Pajek, we would type the relationships into a notepad program and it would look like **Figure D-4.** You represent each person with a number and then list him or her on the same line with his or her link. Vertices is the part of the file that codes each person with a number. The Arcslist shows the relationships that exist.

Figure D-3

Names	Smith	Vargas	Jackson	Wang
Smith	X	1	1	1
Vargas	0	X	1	0
Jackson	1	0	X	1
Wang	0	0	1	X

Figure D-4

```
*Vertices 4
1 "Smith"
2 "Vargas"
3 "Jackson"
4 "Wang"
*Arcslist
1 2 3 4
2 3
3 1 4
4 3
```

When the data are in this format, they can be visualized using social network software by opening it and drawing, as shown in **Figure D-5.** If you look at the arrows leading from Vargas, Smith and Wang, you can see they point to Jackson, meaning they all sit on his board. That means the group's strongest link is to Jackson.

Figure D-5

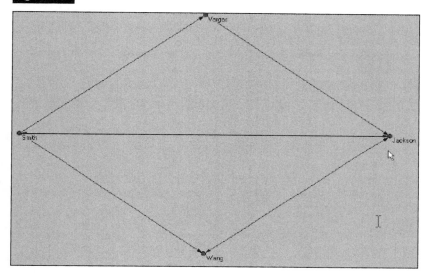

This approach can be used not only for investigations, but simply to understand relationships and connections. IRE programmer and consultant Paul Walmsley used downloaded data from the Securities and Exchange Commission to examine the board of media company Gannett Inc. He wanted to see who sat on Gannett's board and what other boards they sat on to understand the kinds of influences on the management of Gannett. **Figure D-6** shows the diagram of just some of the Gannett board (the data may have changed since the publication of this book).

Figure D-6

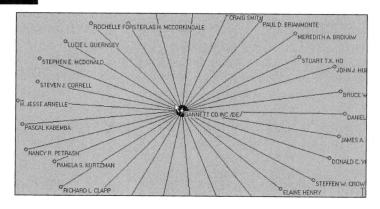

Walmsley added SEC information on more companies, and the result was the illustration in **Figure D-7,** which makes it easy to see other corporate interests and activities of some of Gannett's board.

Figure D-7

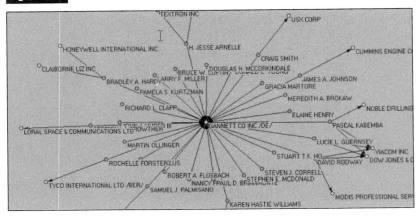

Depending on the dataset and the analysis, social network analysis maps can go far beyond the diagrams shown so far. Experts use mathematical techniques to determine the importance of a person or entity in a network and also to measure the distance and closeness of relationships. You could see how many degrees of separation there are.

Even basic use of this analysis method can be helpful in understanding how decisions and policies are made. It shows how people interact and what patterns evolve through these interactions, which is what journalists observe and write about every day.

By applying these techniques to your community, you could start to more closely track who knows whom, who is isolated from the powerful and who is related to whom. With a better understanding of the relationships, you could ask more probing questions or even prepare better for a routine interview.

▷ **Glossary**

Address   The location on a worksheet identified by a letter and a number.

Ascending   Sorting low to high.

ASCII   American Standard Code for Information Interchange. Pronounced *ask-key*. A file that looks like a text file and can be read by almost any software program.

Average   Usually means the total amount divided by the number of items making up the amount, but in math can refer to mean, median and mode.

Bit   The smallest unit of measuring data and thought of as a 1 or 0.

Boolean logic   A way of searching online and in database managers that used the words *and, or* and *not* to filter information.

BPI   (bits per second) — Used to count the rate of transfer online.

Browser   Software that allows you to see and read Web pages.

Byte   A measure of the amount of space that data takes up on a hard drive. It is composed of eight bits.

CD-ROM   A disk that contains about 600 megabytes; used for storage of data.

Cell   In a spreadsheet, a box containing information.

Codebook   A document translating codes in a database.

Columns   Categories of information in a worksheet.

Computer-assisted reporting   Finding and using databases as a part of the reporting process.

Database   A file or collection of related files.

Database manager   A software program that organizes information in a database.

Descending   Sorting high to low.

Dirty data   Data that have been incorrectly entered into a dataset through typos or miscoding.

Disk/diskette   A storage device for data.

Downloading   To transfer files to your own computer from a computer you have contacted online.

EBCDIC   (Extended Binary Coded Decimal Interchange Code) — Pronounced *eb-see-dic*. A file coded in mainframe language that must be converted to ASCII to be read on a personal computer.

E-mail   Messages sent online.

Enterprise matchmaking   Joining databases that have not been set up to be joined.

Field   A category of information like a column.

File transfer protocol (FTP)   A program language that permits a user to transfer a file from one computer to another.

Filter   To select a subset of numbers from a larger set.

Folders   A place on a computer where files of similar information are stored.

FROM statement   A statement that chooses which database or table to look at.

GROUP BY statement   A statement that divides records into groups based on identical fields.

Grouping   Dividing similar data into groups.

HAVING statement   A statement that selects records after they have been grouped.

Homepage   The starting point on a Web site.

Hypertext   Text files that highlight words. When clicking on the highlighted word known as a link, the user is transferred to another file or page on the Web.

ID number   A key field in a database.

Internet   A vast, worldwide, loosely arranged network of computers.

Lexis/Nexis   A large commercial database of newspaper clippings and court cases.

Listserv   A discussion group on the Internet on a particular topic. All messages sent to the listserv go to all those who have joined.

Log off   To tell a computer that you have finished using it.

Log on   To identify yourself as an authorized user of a computer or Web site.

Mainframe   A large, powerful computer usually kept in an isolated room.

Mapping software   Software that produces maps by matching templates, such as street addresses, to data files imported into the software.

Matches/hits   Finding identical information in the key fields of two or more files.

Mean   The same as average.

Median   The middle value in a series of numbers.

Memory   The storage space in a computer, generally referring to temporary work space known as RAM.

Mode   The number most often occurring in a series of numbers.

Newsgroups   An e-mail group (reached through the Internet) that is formed to discuss a particular topic where messages are posted to be read.

Observation   A record in statistical software.

Offensive characters   Symbols in data that are neither letters nor numbers.

ORDER BY statement   A statement that sorts the records based on one or more fields.

Outlier   Numbers at the extreme of a series of numbers.

Parsing   Dividing a column into one or more columns.

PC   Personal computer; usually refers to an IBM-compatible computer.

Percentage   The proportion of one number to another.

Percentage difference   A proportion of change between two columns of numbers.

Pivot Table   A table of information that allows you to both total numbers in different groups and calculate the percentage of the total those numbers make up.

Query   A way to select, filter, group and sort information in a database.

RAM   Random access memory that acts as temporary work space on a computer.

Rates   The number of occurrences divided by the population in which the occurrences happen.

Ratio   One number divided by another to give a sense of proportion.

Record   A row of information in a database manager.

Record layout   Information about the names and size of fields in a database.

Relational databases   Databases composed of tables that can be joined through "key fields."

Rows   Individual records in a worksheet.

Search   Looking for particular records in a database based on a certain criterion.

Search tool   A program that allows you to search for information on the Internet.

Searchers   Experts who know how to find information on the Internet.

Select   Choosing which columns to look at in a database.

SELECT statement   A statement in SQL that selects the fields to look at.

Sort   Organizing data from high to low, based on information in a column.

Spreadsheet   Software program used for calculations, budgets and other number-related tasks.

SQL   (Structured Query Language) A language used for doing queries in a database and reorganizing and recoding data.

String function   Programming that cleans up dirty data by standardizing a series of letters or numbers.

Summary data   Data that have been divided into groups and totaled.

Tables   Files used by database managers.

Tabular   Information in a table of columns and rows.

URL   (Uniform Resource Locator) The address of a Web site.

Variable   A category of information in statistical software.

WHERE statement   A statement in SQL that selects the records to look at.

Windows   A widely used Microsoft operating system for personal computers.

World Wide Web   A service on the Internet that allows users to use text, sound, graphics and video, and to link these resources to each other.

Zip   To compress a file so that information can be stored and transferred more efficiently.

▷ Bibliography

Babbie, Earl, "The Practice of Social Research," Ninth Edition, Wadsworth Inc., 2000.

Callahan, Christopher, "A Journalist's Guide to the Internet: The Net as Reporting Tool," Second Edition, Pearson Education, 2002.

Cohen, Sarah, "Numbers in the Newsroom," Investigative Reporters and Editors Beat Book Series, 2001.

Cohn, Victor, "News and Numbers," Second Edition, Iowa State University Press, 2001.

Garrison, Bruce, "Computer-Assisted Reporting," Second Edition, Lawrence Erlbaum Associates Inc., 1998.

Hane, Paula, "Super Searchers in the News," Cyberage Books, 2000.

Houston, Brant, Len Bruzzese, and Steven Weinberg, "The Investigative Reporter's Handbook," Fourth Edition, Bedford/St. Martin's, 2002.

Huff, Darrell, "How to Lie with Statistics," W. W. Norton, 1993.

Meyer, Philip, "Precision Journalism," Fourth Edition, Rowman and Littlefield Publishers, 2002.

McGinty, Jo Craven, "Home Mortgage Lending: How to Detect Disparities," Investigative Reporters and Editors Beat Book Series, 2000.

Monmonier, Mark, "How to Lie with Maps," Second Edition, University of Chicago Press, 1996.

National Institute for Computer-Assisted Reporting, "Uplink Collections," Investigative Reporters and Editors, 1999–2002.

Paul, Nora M., "Computer-Assisted Research," Fourth Edition, Bonus Books/Poynter, 1999.

Paul, Nora, and Margot Williams, "Great Scouts!" Cyberage Books, 1999.

Paulos, John Allen, "Beyond Innumeracy," Vintage Books, 1992.

Reddick, Randy, and Elliot King, "The Online Journalist," Third Edition, Harcourt College, 2000.

Schlein, Alan, "Find It Online," Facts on Demand Press, 2000.

Simon, Joel, with Carol Napolitano, "We're All Nerds Now," *Columbia Journalism Review,* April 1999.

Silver, Kurt, "Understanding Crime Statistics: A Reporter's Guide," Investigative Reporters and Editors Beat Book Series, 2001.

Tessier, Marie, "Covering Aviation Safety: An Investigator's Guide," Investigative Reporters and Editors Beat Book Series, 2000.

Tufte, Edward, "Envisioning Information," Graphics Press, 1990.

Acknowledgments

Figures 2.6–2.9: Screenshots from www.Google.com. Reprinted by permission.

Figure 2.11: Screenshot of "Annex Table 4 Healthy Life Expectancy (HALE) in All Member States, Estimates for 2000" from World Health Organization Web site, "The World Health Report 2001," www.who.int/whr2001/2001/main/ennex/annex4-en-WEB.xls. Copyright © 2001 by World Health Organization. Reprinted by permission.

Figure 2.15: Screenshot of "Healthy Life Expectancy: The World Health Report 2001" from World Health Organization WHOSIS Web site, www3.who.int/whosis/hale/halecfm?path=whosis.burden_statistics.hale& language=english. Copyright © 2001 by World Health Organization. Reprinted by permission.

Figure 2.16: Screenshot of "Annex Table 4 Healthy Life Expectancy (HALE) in All Member States, Estimates for 2000" from World Health Organization Web site, "The World Health Report 2001," www.who.int/whr2001/2001/main/ennex/annex4-en-WEB.xls. Copyright © 2001 by World Health Organization. Reprinted by permission.

Screenshots from SPSS database. Copyright © by SPSS, Inc., Chicago. Reprinted with permission.

Screenshots from ArcView. Copyright © 2003 by ESRI. All rights reserved.

Figure D.1: Diagram of relationships between terrorists involved in 2001 World Trade Center attacks from Valdis E. Krebs, "Uncloaking Terrorist Networks" in First Monday 7, no. 1 (April 2002), http://firstmonday.org/issues/issue7_4/krebs/, Figure 4. Copyright © 2002 by Valdis E. Krebs. Reprinted with permission.

▷ Index

242